# JIM CORBETT

## MASTER OF THE JUNGLE

# JIM CORBETT

## MASTER OF THE JUNGLE

*by*
*Tim Werling*

## SAFARI PRESS INC.

P.O. BOX 3095, LONG BEACH, CALIFORNIA 90803

Werling, Tim

First edition

Safari Press Inc.

1998, Long Beach, California

ISBN 1-57157-104-3

Library of Congress Catalog Card Number: 97-69553

10 9 8 7 6 5 4 3 2 1

Readers wishing to receive the Safari Press catalog, featuring many fine books on big-game hunting, wingshooting, and sporting firearms, should write to Safari Press Inc., P.O. Box 3095, Long Beach, CA 90803, USA. Tel: (714) 894-9080 or visit our Web site at www.safaripress.com.

# CONTENTS

# CONTENTS

# AUTHOR'S NOTE

*During the early 1900s, an estimated 40,000 tigers stalked the forests in India. Today, only about 2,500 of these magnificent animals remain in India's wild. What caused this tragedy?*

Some believe the tiger's demise in India was caused by the slaughter during the British Raj. This period in history was renown for the big-game hunter and British, Indian royalty, and others sought to prove their mettle by shooting a tiger in India. Because of the tiger's proliferation, the bag limit was often great. Nevertheless, this was not the principal reason for the tiger's current plight.

Tiger environment, or lack thereof, is the main reason the largest predatory cat in the world is near extinction. Overpopulation in India, Russia (Siberia), China, and Southeast Asia has forced the tiger into smaller, more remote, and less desirable areas to live. As a result, the tigers reproduce less, and eliminate each other as they vie for territory that contains only minimal natural prey. Attacks on humans by completely healthy tigers are becoming more prevalent, as the tigers' natural food supply dwindles.

By the late 1960s, approximately 1,800 tigers remained in India. Aware of this dilemma, India instituted a program in 1973 called "Project Tiger." The government of India and the World Wildlife Fund have donated funds to create and maintain tiger reserves throughout India. The initial reserve was established in Garhwal District, Kumaon Division, and was named after Jim Corbett. Additionally, the tiger has been placed on the "endangered species" list, making it illegal to hunt tigers. Many countries, including the United States, prohibit importing tiger skins or parts.

Project Tiger was a resounding success until recently. By the late 1980s, the tiger population in India had reportedly doubled to over four thousand. However, due to the insatiable demand for tiger parts, poaching in India's tiger preserves has reduced the tiger population significantly. Asians, who use and consume tiger parts for a variety of medicinal and aphrodisiac reasons, are willing to pay exorbitant prices for these exotic animals. Unfortunately, to many Indians, the financial rewards for dealing in tiger parts outweighs the risk of getting caught.

Our only hope for the tiger's survival in the wild is for people throughout the world to recognize its plight, and ensure tigers are allocated the territory and protection they require. Without either, the tiger is destined for extinction. Our world would certainly be a lesser place if the tiger could never again roar its fearsome call in the wild.

*Note: Jim Corbett was granted "freedom of the forests" in India, a privilege only given to one other person before. In 1957, the Indian government named a tiger preserve in Garhwal District after him as a tribute to his humanitarian effort to the natives of Kumaon.*

# CHRONOLOGY OF JIM CORBETT'S LIFE

*Date*          *Event*

25 July 1875.....Born in Naini Tal, India, to Christopher William and Mary Jane Corbett.

1881.................Father died of heart failure at age 59.

1893.................Began employment as fuel inspector at Mankapur or the Bengal and North Western Railway. Later, was transferred to Mokameh Ghat in Bengal, where he supervised a labor force for 20 years as a materials transshipment supervisor.

1899.................Younger brother Archie dies at age 20.

1907.................Destroyed his first man-eating tiger at Champawat, which had killed 436 humans.

1914-1918........Joined British forces during WWI and was commissioned as a captain. Recruited a labor force of 5,000 Indians from his homeland, 500 of whom he took with him to France.

1919-1921........Served at the rank of major in the Waziristan campaign in the North West Frontier in India, where he commanded the 114th Labor Battalion in the Third Afghan War.

1922.................Began spending part of each year for the next 15 years in Tanganyika, Africa, where he hunted big game and helped supervise his jointly owned coffee plantation.

1924..............Mother passed away.

1930..............Shot the famed "Bachelor of Powalgarh,"
the most prized tiger of the decade.
Attitude toward hunting changes.
He still hunted for sport, but moderately,
and became more of a conservationist.

1938..............Destroyed the Thak tiger.

1939-1945.... Appointed as Deputy Military vice-president
of District Soldiers Boards, tasked to
organize a civil pioneer corps during WWII.
Later, was promoted to lieutenant colonel,
and trained British soldiers in jungle warfare.

1940..............Published his first book, *Jungle Stories*.

1946............. *Man-eaters of Kumaon,* revised edition of
*Jungle Stories,* is published worldwide and
becomes a best-seller.

1947..............India gained independence. Jim and sister
Maggie left India and settled in Nyeri,
Kenya, Africa.

1948-1955....Published five more books from his memoirs:
*The Man-eating Leopard of Rudraprayag,*
*The Temple Tiger, My India, Jungle Lore,*
and *Tree Tops.*

1955..............Died of heart failure and buried in Africa.

# ACKNOWLEDGMENTS

I owe a debt of gratitude to many people who provided me with support and assistance throughout this endeavor. I wish to offer special thanks to the following individuals: my mother, Dorothy, for giving me a copy of Jim Corbett's *Man-eaters of Kumaon,* thus inspiring me to write this story; my wife, Susan, for her steadfast support and encouragement; Ludo Wurfbain and Dr. Jacqueline Neufeld at Safari Press for their expert advice and guidance, and the opportunity to make this a reality; my son, Dan, for his technical support; Oxford University Press personnel for permission to use material from Jim Corbett's books; Peter Byrne, Paul Roberts, and David Marx for providing photos; and the library staff at the U.S. Air Force Academy for helping me locate applicable reference material. Thank you all!

# DEDICATION

*For Susan*
*And to the memory of Jim Corbett of Kumaon.*

# PREFACE

Imagine what it must have been like as a child born during the early 1930s in a small village located in the forested foothills of northern India. Ignorant of the ways of modern society, you are taught everything by your parents and other villagers, who are simple people scratching out an existence from nature's bounty. You live in a small mud-and-thatch hut with no indoor plumbing or electricity. You have virtually no clothes to wear, and your knowledge of the world extends only a short distance beyond the boundaries of your village.

As such, you are told about the spirits that guide your daily life—the spirits in the land, water, and forest. You are also told about the animals in the forest; which ones are safe, and which ones are dangerous. You learn that the tiger is the guardian of the forest and commands respect. It is a solitary animal with long, sharp fangs and claws that normally preys on other animals of the forest. Despite its size, it can move through the forest like a shadow, and appear out of nowhere. You are told that if you offend any of the spirits, the tiger may seek revenge to appease the wronged spirit. You begin having nightmares about the "monster" in the forest, which stalks you relentlessly in your sleep.

Then one day, a large tiger attacks and carries away one of the village women who was gathering sticks near the edge of the forest. Several men in the village grab their homemade weapons and, as a group, run to the attack site in an attempt to retrieve the woman.

When they return an hour later, they are carrying the remains of the woman. They place her on the ground for all to see. You gaze in horror at what was, only an hour ago, one of your close neighbors. Most of her clothes have been torn from her body. Her remaining tattered clothes are saturated with blood. Her left leg is missing, severed from her upper thigh. Blood is trickling from large puncture holes in her neck, and long lacerations extend from her right shoulder down her back. Her face is covered with dirt and leaves, which have stuck to the coagulating blood.

Her husband is sitting next to her mutilated body, staring in disbelief. And, her three small children are standing nearby, sobbing over the loss of their mother. Your mother ushers you back into your house, to protect you from the grisly scene. You overhear some of the villagers discussing what transgression the woman could have committed to be attacked and killed by a tiger.

Two days later, your sister is attacked by a tiger while gathering fodder for the cattle. You are standing only fifty feet away from her when you hear her piercing scream. You watch in horror as the huge, tawny beast carries her into the forest. For several minutes, you are too frightened to move. You are frozen with fear. Suddenly, your father grabs you and carries you back to the village. Your father, along with several other men, returns to the area to search for your sister. Fifteen minutes later, they come back to the village running as fast as they can.

When order resumes, they begin to accuse each other of being the first to run when the tiger charged at them from a thicket. When their voices subside, no one is willing to accompany your father back to the forest. Your father goes alone.

Thirty minutes later, your father returns without your sister. He holds your weeping mother in his arms and tells her he found some blood in the thicket, but, he saw no sign of your sister or the tiger. You never see your sister again.

Over the next six months, the tiger continues to attack and kill other villagers. Some of the bodies are recovered; some are not. Everyone in the village is terrorized by the recurring onslaught. The villagers hope desperately the offended spirit will soon be appeased, so the killing will stop. But, the attacks continue. Everyone feels helpless, and the situation appears hopeless.

Nearly every family within the village has lost at least one of their family members to the tiger. Everyone in the village is afraid to leave their huts, even during the day. The sanitary condition of the village deteriorates significantly. Human feces continue to accumulate in the village courtyard. Those who are too afraid to leave their huts have no choice but to urinate and defecate inside. The stench from human waste during the hot daylight hours is nauseating.

Food is becoming scarce. The tiger has taken the few goats and buffalo that belonged to your father, and the crops in the fields adjoining the village are being ravaged by birds and other animals. Your father, along with other village men, forages for fruit and nuts close to the village. Each time he returns, he brings back less food to eat. The men also journey to the nearby stream every few days to obtain water. If someone sees or has recently seen the tiger, everyone stays within their huts until enough courage is mustered to venture outside again.

No one visits your village anymore because of the tiger's tyranny. The village headman communicates to people in a nearby village by standing on a large boulder next to his hut and shouting at the top of his lungs. He is informed that the tiger has killed many people within their village also.

As people become more wary of the tiger, the beast becomes bolder in its attempts to find human prey. Some nights, you can hear it moaning softly as it moves with sinister stealth throughout the village. Your father keeps the thatched windows and door closed tightly at night, barricading the door with additional sticks for security.

One night you hear the tiger clawing at the side of your hut. Your mother screams hysterically, frightened out of her wits. You huddle with your father and mother on the floor, shivering in terror—afraid to fall asleep. You are living under a man-eater's tyranny, terrified you will become its next victim. Your worst nightmare has become real!

The preceding dramatization is not only frightening, but true. Many people who lived in tiger and leopard infested areas throughout Asia succumbed to such terror. In fact, many people are still killed by tigers today, especially in the Sunderbans region in northeastern India.

Despite all the efforts taken by the Indian government to separate tigers from people, the human death toll increases each year as people continue to venture into tiger territory.

Injury or old age are the usual reasons these large cats resort to stalking humans as prey. Nevertheless, once they adapt to hunting humans, they continue their reign of terror until they are destroyed or die of old age. Tigers normally live a life of solitude, except for periods of mating. Occasionally, they will share a "kill," but usually wait their turn until the other tiger has eaten its share from the carcass. Requiring large quantities of flesh to satisfy its hunger, an adult tiger will often consume up to seventy pounds during a meal. Not knowing where and when it will obtain its next meal, tigers gorge themselves whenever possible.

Despite its stealth, even healthy tigers are successful in only one out of every twenty attacks. Therefore, when injury or age hinders their speed, tigers resort to preying on smaller animals, wresting prey from other predators, and sometimes becoming man-eaters. Like man, tigers have a strong spirit of survival. As such, they too will alter their diet to stay alive.

This story is about a courageous man who risked his own life to protect and save the lives of native villagers in India, who found themselves living under a man-eater's tyranny. Jim

Corbett's vast knowledge and experience of the animals he hunted were the only advantages he had when he set out to stalk one of these beasts in their natural environment. Tracking a five-hundred-pound tiger through dense, hilly forest and rocky terrain would be unnerving enough. Knowing the ferocious predator had killed and devoured scores of human beings, and one careless mistake would put you at its mercy, only added to the tension of bringing the man-eater to justice.

Jim Corbett's book, *Man-eaters of Kumaon*, first published in 1944, by Oxford University Press, was the inspiration for this book. *Jim Corbett—Master of the Jungle*, while rooted in fact from actual accounts of Corbett's hunts after man-eating tigers and leopards, has been creatively interpreted.

Corbett was born in northern India in 1875, and he spent most of his youth in the forest, studying wildlife and learning to hunt. Blessed with keen eyesight and an accurate aim, he became a marksman of unequaled stature. From 1907 to 1938, Corbett destroyed several man-eating tigers and leopards throughout the Kumaon Hills. Although difficult to determine exactly how many lives he had saved, two man-eaters were known to have each killed over four hundred people before Corbett was able to destroy them. This is the story of a brave and extraordinary man.

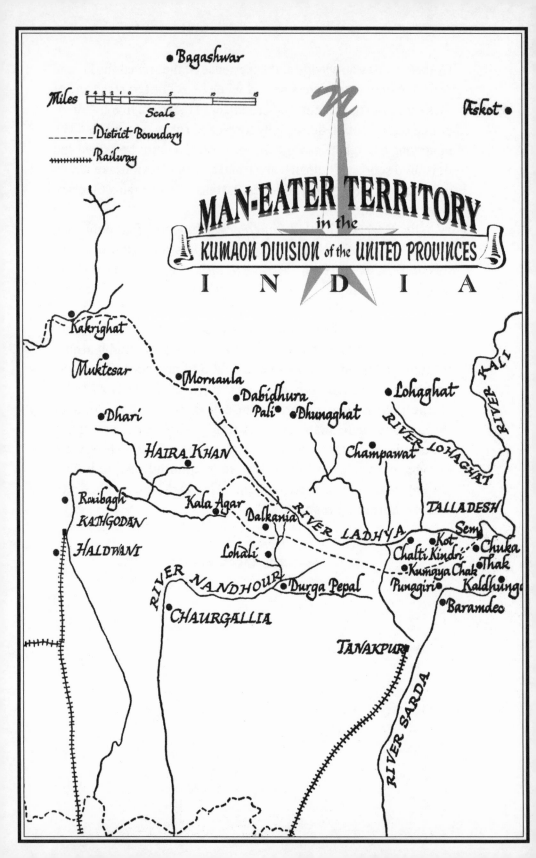

*Beauteous is Earth, but all its forests broods—*
*Plot mutual slaughter, hungering to live.*
*Sir Edwin Arnold, "The Light of Asia"*

April 19, 1890, near Sem Village, Kumaon Division of the United Provinces, Northern India.

The bone snapped like a parched twig. Blood oozed from the severed limb onto the dry, matted grass. The tigress licked the blood from the exposed flesh, then sank her fangs deep into the buttocks of the carcass and tore off a large portion of flesh. She chewed the fresh, warm meat three times, then swallowed hard.

A red squirrel sitting in a tree at the edge of the nearby forest chattered its alarm. The tigress lifted her head and cocked her ears forward, listening intently. She heard human voices. Seconds later, she heard their footsteps padding closer along the forest path from where she had just come. She lay still, ever alert to man's presence.

The stocky Irish hunter, Reginald Donahue, stopped at the edge of the forest. He signaled his two Indian porters to halt and remain quiet. The hunter handed his polished double-barreled rifle to the nearest porter, then reached inside the left breast pocket of his short-sleeved khaki jacket and pulled out a large red handkerchief. He mopped the perspiration from his face and neck, then crouched down to examine the tiger's pug marks in the soft earth.

"Sahib," the porter remarked as he pointed, "it went into the grass."

The big man stood up and sighed as he stuffed the kerchief back into his pocket. He removed the tan safari hat from his head and scratched the back of his bald head while sizing up the situation.

The large field to his front contained thick elephant grass nearly ten feet tall. Approximately fifty yards wide and seventy-five yards deep, it sloped gently away from them until it abutted a rocky ravine containing a stream. The field was surrounded on the three other sides by forest consisting mostly of scrub oak brush and tall pine and spruce trees.

"Ten thousand damnations upon you!" the hunter muttered in his Irish brogue. He picked up a large rock and hurled it deep into the field. "Come out of there, you striped fiend of Hell!"

His puffy crimson face was flushed with rage. He slapped the side of his right knee where a black fly was feasting. The exposed flesh between the top of his gray, wool stockings, which were pulled up over the calf, and the cuff of his khaki shorts was covered with welts from tormenting insects. The two porters looked at each other, both afraid to say anything for fear of offending the burly Irishman.

The hunter scanned the terrain bordering the field, searching for a vantage point high enough so that he would be safe from attack and gain a view into the field. There was none. The grass was too tall and too thick. He glanced over at the porter holding his rifle.

"Why d'ye look at me like that?" he growled accusingly. "You go in there and flush it out!" He gestured toward the field.

"No, Sahib!" the porter exclaimed apologetically. "I no hunt!"

"Then go boil your head, you rotter. You are of no use to either man or beast!" He snatched the rifle from the Indian's hands. "I'm going back to camp."

He turned toward the field, shook his fist, and shouted: "You striped devil—I'll get ye yet!"

The tigress listened to the men's footsteps become more and more faint. Satisfied that the men were a safe distance away, she resumed her meal. She ate the intestines, then pulled the stomach from the body cavity and ate it next.

When the tigress had consumed fifty pounds of flesh, her hunger was satisfied. The flies, which now covered the carcass's remains, were beginning to torment the tigress. She rose and walked slowly to the stream, where she could quench her thirst and clean herself. She would then find a secluded spot deep in the forest where she could rest. In two days she would be hungry again and have to hunt for more prey. It was a matter of survival. She had to hunt and kill to stay alive.

Three vultures descended onto the carrion lying in the field. One began to pick at the young girl's eyes and blood-soaked black hair. The tigress did not leave much for the scavengers, but they were thankful for any morsels they could find.

The following day, the hunter returned to the field with four British hunters. Enlisting the help of seventeen elephants and eighty-five local villagers, they conducted a "beat" from one end of the grassy field to the other, hoping to drive the tigress to the armed hunters waiting at the far end. All they found were the victim's pitiful remains, which were returned to the parents. The grieving parents were thankful for the scant remains, for now they could perform for their only daughter the customary cremation ceremony on the riverbank near the village.

---

Headquarters, Volunteer Rifles Company, Naini Tal District, United Provinces, Northern India.

The half-inch-thick rattan cane swished through the sultry air and left its mark on the purple welts made by previous strokes.

"Six!" the young recipient blubbered.

"How many?" the elderly sergeant shouted.

"Six, Sergeant!" The boy grimaced, waiting for the next stroke. Sweat dripped from his flushed face onto the worn, wooden plank floor—more from the heat and humidity than from the searing pain. The wiry sergeant slapped the cane down hard onto the top of the scarred oak desk next to him, then walked around the desk and sat in his equally weathered chair.

"Six will be it for today, Mister Corbett. Next time, you'll receive a dozen."

Jim Corbett removed his hands from his knees and pulled up the dark blue uniform shorts as he stood erect. He tucked the matching-colored shirttails into his shorts, buttoned his fly, and buckled the wide brown leather belt.

"Did you learn anything from today's mischief, Mister Corbett?" the sergeant asked as he straightened some paperwork on the desk.

"Aye, Sergeant," Jim replied as he pushed his long, sandy-colored hair away from his face. "Don't get caught."

Jim's face was flushed and his eyes still watered.

"You're as hardheaded as I was at your age until my sergeant beat some sense into me. For your sake, lad, I hope you learn faster than I did."

"Aye, Sergeant!" Jim looked into the old soldier's eyes and saw the man's sincerity.

The sergeant harbored no ill will toward Jim. He treated all of his young charges the same. All defaulters in the company could expect a stiff verbal reprimand, followed by a caning upon completion of the day's drill. Everyone in Jim's company had felt the business end of ol' Sarge's cane at one time or another. Jim felt it more than most. But he deserved it. Both he and the sergeant could agree on that.

The procedure was always the same. Anyone who committed an infraction and was marked for a caning would line up outside the sergeant's office following drill. Sarge would call the boys in one at a time and order them to assume the position. The young offender would then lower his britches and bend forward, placing his hands on his knees.

Sarge determined the number of strokes each offender was to receive, based on the seriousness of the infraction. Minor offenses received three strokes; it was six for more serious infractions and a dozen for repeat offenders. Minor offenses normally included reporting for the day's drill with a dirty or torn uniform, or making too many mistakes while marching in formation or while conducting rifle drills. Showing disrespect to a superior or dishonoring the company definitely merited six strokes.

Jim's infraction was attempting to "de-pants" one of his comrades while the boy was adjusting his britches.

"Mister Corbett!" Sarge had bellowed upon catching Jim in the act. "Report to my office after drill!"

Jim's best friend, Kyle Benton, had snickered aloud over the incident and received three strokes.

This was British justice—swift, sure, and always painful. No jury. No discussion. No explanation. And definitely no excuses! Sarge was judge, jury, and executioner. But he was fair, and the boys respected him. At age fifty-three, Sarge was tough as granite. He knew that being posted at Naini Tal was a plum assignment, but he did not take it lightly. He was responsible for turning British and Indian boys between the ages of ten and seventeen into men and, it was hoped, generate enough interest among some to join the military service in India later on.

Jim walked gingerly along the crushed stone path leading from Sarge's small, dusty, sun-bleached, wood-framed office to the rickety gate next to the main dirt road leading to Naini Tal Village. Kyle was at the gate waiting.

"I hope ol' Deadeye gave it to you good, you dumb idiot!" Kyle said as he shoved Jim's shoulder. "It was your fault I had to take a thrashing too."

"Sorry, but I couldn't resist the temptation when Porky was adjusting his shorts."

"Porky," or Portnoy Cairns, was the frequent target of Jim's pranks. Jim detested Porky. Not only was he the son of Lieutenant Cairns, special assistant to the deputy district commissioner, but he was pompous and obnoxious. Porky, like other boys who were the offspring of British officials in India, treated Jim and his ilk like pond scum.

Although Jim's grandparents were "expatriates" (British citizens born in England or Ireland who were posted or migrated to India), Jim and his immediate family were "domiciled" (British citizens who were born in India and, while respected, were not afforded the same social status as expatriates).

Jim's father, Christopher William Corbett, had been appointed as postmaster for Naini Tal by the deputy district commissioner. He had three children from his first marriage to Mary Anne Murrow, who had died prematurely. Jim's mother, the former Mary Jane Doyle, had three surviving children from her previous marriage to Charles James Doyle, who was hacked to death by sword-wielding Indian mutineers in 1858. Mary had saved the meager proceeds from her late husband's life insurance and used it to send the children from her first marriage to England to attend school.

Christopher Corbett married Mary Jane Doyle at Mussoorie in 1859, and they had nine children spaced over eighteen years, of whom Jim was second youngest.

When Christopher Corbett was appointed postmaster, the deputy district commissioner provided him with a land grant at Kaladhungi, which was located fifteen miles south of Naini Tal. The Corbetts spent their winters at a house they had built in Kaladhungi to escape the cold climate. Although the distance between the two locations was minimal, Kaladhungi was about four thousand feet lower in elevation than Naini Tal, making it much more temperate during the winter months.

Jim's father had died of heart failure when Jim was five years old. His meager pension forced Jim's mother, Mary, to pinch every rupee to make ends meet. She rented out half of their house in Naini Tal to bring in needed income, and earned a commission renting houses that were owned by other British residents.

Supporting fifteen children required everyone's participation. The older boys hunted and fished for food, and the girls helped around the house and tended the garden. One of Jim's duties, which he detested, was to escort his sisters to the canal each day for their bath. He had to alert the girls if any men approached.

Clothes were a luxury, and the children had to make do with two changes—one for play and work, and the other for dress. Shoes were not considered a necessity when the children were young.

Only one other European family resided in Kaladhungi, so both families mixed freely with their Indian neighbors. Poverty was the standard fare at Kaladhungi, so the Corbetts felt right at home. Indians were always welcomed at their house, and were treated for almost any ailment they had. At Naini Tal, however, wealthy British families abounded, and the Indian population there was forced to live apart from the "Whites."

Socially, Jim and his family were considered outcasts, only slightly higher than the Anglo-Indian half-castes. As a result, Mary was excluded from many British social functions. Even though Mary wanted desperately to be accepted and respected by her countrymen, she didn't have the time or money to squander on social events.

It wasn't only Mary's social status that precluded her from attracting any suitors. Her disheveled and frumpy appearance, a result of managing a large household single-handedly, was not conducive to turning any heads. "Homely as burlap," a man said of her once. The truth of the matter was, she was.

She always dressed plain, talked plain, and looked plain. Her ash-colored hair was kept neatly tied in a bun at the back of her head, and her hard life made her look old beyond her years. Her income was meager, but she accepted her lot in life without complaint and did the best she could to keep her family intact.

Mary's patience, perseverance, and hard-work ethic were passed to Jim and his siblings. With Mary's enormous responsibilities, Jim was forced to fend for himself as he grew up. Raised in such an environment and snubbed by British society, it was no surprise that the Corbetts identified and socialized more with their Indian neighbors.

"Deadeye was right on the mark again," commented Jim as he winced in pain. "Deadeye," Sarge's nickname, had an uncanny knack of laying the cane directly across the welts left from his previous strokes. This, of course, not only intensified the pain during the caning but also took a longer time to heal.

Kyle laughed, forcing Jim to smile. Then he said, "I'm meeting Tommie at the river fork in a half-hour to hunt pheasant. You want to come along?"

"No, I'll go straight home. I've got chores to do. Anyway, we still have some birds from yesterday that we haven't eaten."

"Right, then, I'll see you tomorrow." Kyle playfully punched Jim's shoulder again and ran off toward his house. He was three inches shorter than Jim's six-foot frame but was ten pounds heavier.

Jim was lanky and slightly uncoordinated for his fifteen years, but his keen senses compensated for his physical flaws. Although he was only average in his school subjects, Jim was the pride of the company when it came to marksmanship. When hunting with Kyle and Tommie, Jim consistently brought home the largest bag.

Jim loved the forest, and had spent most of his spare time since he was five years old wandering along the forest paths studying the sights and sounds of nature's bounty. When he was twelve, he became so enthralled with the numerous species of birds that he categorized them into six groups: 1) birds that beautify nature's garden, such as orioles and sunbirds; 2) birds of melody, such as thrushes and robins; 3) birds that regenerate the garden, such as barbets, hornbills, and bulbuls; 4) birds that warn of danger, such as jungle fowl and bablers; 5) birds that maintain the balance of nature, such as eagles, hawks, and owls; and 6) scavengers such as vultures and crows. He became so familiar with most species that he could identify a bird not only by its sound but even by its nests and eggs.

Jim was at peace in the forest; he preferred solitude to company. He learned how to stalk game quietly, and practiced sneaking up on animals just to see how close he could get before they became aware of his presence.

One day when Jim was twelve, he was returning home from the forest near Kaladhungi, whistling the call of a thrush. As he passed an Indian man smoking a *buree* (cigar) at the side of the path, the Indian answered back at Jim with his own thrush imitation. Upon hearing the "thrush," Jim stopped and looked around for the bird. As he did so, the man began laughing. The Indian then imitated the call of a peafowl.

Jim was impressed. He had never heard anyone imitate the calls so realistically. Jim sat next to the man and, for the next two hours, traded bird calls with him. Each time the man whistled a call, Jim tried to emulate. Jim was accurate with most of the simple calls but had difficulty with the complicated ones. When Jim rose to his feet to return home, the man beckoned him to remain seated.

"Close your eyes and listen carefully," he ordered. Jim sat and listened intently.

The man whispered, "You are deep in the forest—lost. It's dark, and you have to stay the night." He then began making the eerie sounds of the forest at twilight. Beginning with several bird calls, he progressed to the monkeys and deer. Jim was enthralled. Then the man was silent for several seconds. Suddenly, he gave the alarm call of a spotted chital deer, followed by a langur monkey. This was followed by the low, guttural, warning growl of a tiger. Jim shuddered nervously. The Indian repeated the throaty growl, waited a few seconds, then roared ferociously like a tiger attacking its prey.

*"Ahhhh!"* Jim yelled as his eyes popped open. They were as big as saucers, reflecting mortal fear.

The Indian broke out in laughter, slapping Jim on the leg. The Indian's wife, who overheard the incident, chided her husband for scaring Jim out of his wits.

On his way home, Jim kept looking back at the Indian, marveling at his unique gift. He had never known anyone who could imitate animal sounds so effectively. Jim knew he would be returning for many more lessons. He was hooked. Little did he know how valuable those lessons would become.

Over the next eight months, Jim and the Indian were inseparable. The Indian, known as Kunwah Singh, was an expert tracker. But what really endeared him to Jim was the fact that Kunwah was a notorious poacher—a person from whom Jim could learn many things. Often Kunwah and Jim went into the nearby forest, where Kunwah taught Jim how to identify animal tracks.

It wasn't long before Jim could not only identify the animals by their tracks but also tell which direction they were headed, how recently they'd passed, their approximate weight, how fast they were going, and in some cases their sex. Kunwah tested Jim constantly, whenever they came across a track. When they found fresh tracks, the two stalked the animal until they located it. They were successful almost always, unless the animal traveled over rocky terrain or for a considerable distance through water.

"If you want to be a good hunter," Kunwah advised, "you have to learn to see with your ears."

"What do you mean?" Jim asked.

"You must learn to depend on your hearing more than your sight. When you are in the forest, stop often and listen to the sounds. Most humans make too much noise in the forest and rely too much on their sight. That is why most of them cannot hunt well. The animals hear them coming long before they are within shooting range, and run away or hide. Now, close your eyes and tell me what you hear."

Jim closed his eyes and tuned in his hearing. "I just hear the normal sounds—birds chirping and singing, monkeys chattering. . . ."

"What does that tell you?"

"That everything is normal. Nothing is upsetting the animals."

"Right. Now let us walk farther."

When they had covered another one hundred yards, Kunwah stopped. "Close your eyes and listen again."

Jim listened intently to similar sounds, as before, but this time he was able to discern the faint alarm call of a spotted chital deer in the distance.

"I hear a chital's alarm," he announced proudly.

"Yes. In what direction?"

"Over there." Jim pointed northeast.

"Correct. How far?"

"Maybe 150 or 200 yards."

"Good. What has alarmed the chital?"

"Most likely a tiger or leopard. However, since leopards hunt mostly at night, it is probably a tiger."

"Very good. Keep listening and tell me which way the tiger is moving and how fast it is traveling."

"How can I tell that?"

"Listen!" A few seconds later, Jim heard the alarm call of a langur monkey about the same distance away, but farther north than the chital.

"*Ahhh*! The tiger is heading north. Judging from the time between the alarm calls, I would say it is walking at a slow pace."

"Excellent! You have learned today's lesson well."

When Jim had honed his expertise sufficiently, Kunwah decided it was time to let him track a tiger. One day when they came across fresh tiger pug marks, Jim got his opportunity. After Jim correctly identified the tiger's sex, direction, rate of travel, and roughly how recently it had passed by, Kunwah gave him the lead to track it. A short distance later, Kunwah noticed a line in the dirt next to the tiger's pug marks. He explained to a puzzled Jim that the line was the drag mark from the tiger's recent kill.

"Why are there no traces of blood?" Jim asked.

"The tiger is still gripping its kill by its initial hold," Kunwah explained. "If the tiger changes its hold, then blood will flow from the initial holes made by the tiger's fangs."

Jim was fascinated and eager to pursue the tracking. Kunwah had to caution Jim on several occasions to slow down and be more quiet.

"Tigers have excellent sight and can hear sounds that we cannot," Kunwah whispered. "If you want to see the tiger before it sees or hears you, you must become part of the forest." Jim nodded as Kunwah continued. "We must be careful. If the tiger thinks we are trying to steal its food, it may attack us!" Upon hearing *that* remark, Jim decided to allow Kunwah to take the lead.

Kunwah and his student cautiously tracked the tiger for more than a mile through dense forest, finally approaching a deep ravine containing a small stream. Kunwah signaled Jim to lie down.

"The tiger's in the ravine," Kunwah stated.

Jim whispered, "How can you tell?"

"The tracks lead in that direction, and the tiger will want to drink after it eats." Kunwah held his hand up. "Listen!"

The two listened carefully for several seconds, then heard the crunching sound of the tiger chewing through bone. Slowly and quietly they crawled to the edge of the ravine to get a better view. When they reached the edge, they peered down, focusing in the direction of the noise. It was coming from some thick bushes next to the stream. Occasionally, the tiger growled in frustration when it encountered difficulty with its prey. Jim and Kunwah watched intently, trying to get a glimpse of the tiger.

Suddenly, it growled again. A bush shook, and something red and brown extended out from the foliage, agitating violently. It was a portion of the prey. As it quickly disappeared back into the bushes, Jim gasped in horror. He turned to look at Kunwah, who also had a startled look in his eyes. They could not believe what they had seen, but there was no doubt: it was a *human* leg.

Kunwah put his finger to his lips and beckoned at Jim to crawl back from the edge. As Jim moved his leg, however, he snapped a small twig with his knee. Horrified, they remained motionless. Kunwah knew that if the tiger had heard the noise, it would do one of two things: run away or investigate. If it ran away, the chance to destroy it when he returned with a hunter would be diminished. If it investigated, there would probably be no one to fetch the hunter.

Seconds went by like hours. Finally, their nerves screaming with fear, they heard the crunching noise again and breathed a sigh of relief. They continued to inch their way from the ravine until Kunwah thought it was safe to run.

Twenty minutes later, they were at the district deputy commissioner's office, explaining what they had seen. The deputy commissioner had hunted many times with Kunwah and believed his story, despite the fact that no one had reported a tiger attack. Jim was sent home, and Kunwah and the deputy commissioner went after the tiger with four other men.

Three hours later, the entourage returned carrying the dead tiger hanging upside down from a large bamboo pole, its feet were lashed securely to the pole. When they reached the deputy commissioner's office, they placed the tiger on the ground. Kunwah was carrying a small cloth containing the victim's remains—a few bone splinters and a small piece of blood-soaked clothing. A crowd assembled around the tiger as an Indian man began to skin it with his knife. Jim never found out who the victim was. Maybe it was some unfortunate traveler who was at the wrong place at the wrong time. Although Jim would see more grisly scenes in the years to come, he never forgot the image of that bloody leg protruding from the thicket.

Eleven months after the tiger incident, Jim and Kunwah were in the forest imitating animal calls when Jim noticed some snake tracks in the sand along the trail. The tracks indicated that the snake was fairly large and was moving at a fast pace.

"Cobra!" Kunwah announced. "Between ten and twelve feet."

"How can you tell how long . . . ?"

Just then, the reptile charged at them from some thick bushes twenty feet away, its hood expanded. Jim froze in fear. With only seconds to react, Kunwah pushed Jim off to the side. Their feet tangled, causing Kunwah to trip and fall to the ground. Jim was lying only a few feet from Kunwah when he saw the snake strike. Kunwah screamed in pain and reached for his leg. After striking, the cobra quickly slithered back into the forest.

Jim was petrified, afraid to move. Kunwah continued holding his leg, writhing in agony. Finally, he withdrew his hunting knife from its sheath and made two incisions across the wound. "Suck venom. Hurry!" he ordered Jim.

Jim regained his senses and sucked on the bite mark. Several times he spit out the blood and venom he'd extracted from the wound, careful not to swallow any of the deadly poison. He then helped Kunwah to his feet, and they returned to the village as fast as they could.

Kunwah was barely coherent when they arrived at his house. His wife helped Jim carry Kunwah to his bed. When Jim explained what had happened, she swooned. Several other curious villagers, upon hearing the commotion, came running into the house.

Jim immediately ran home for help, returning with his older brother, Tom, who examined the wound carefully. Tom realized that only one of the cobra's fangs had penetrated Kunwah's leg and that the wound, fortunately, was not very deep. He wrapped it with clean cloth and said to Jim and the others standing in the room, "There's nothing more we can do but let him rest and make sure he stays warm."

Jim checked on his old friend every day, and on the sixth day, Kunwah miraculously recovered. He was truly lucky. Since there was no antidote or effective cure for cobra venom at the time, most people who were attacked suffered an agonizing death. Kunwah's unfortunate incident only reinforced Jim's deep respect for and hatred toward snakes.

Despite all the dangers and diseases prevalent in the jungle around Kaladhungi, Kunwah managed to live and hunt for many more years—until he finally succumbed to the vile drug opium.

When Jim approached his house, he saw Maggie, his older sister by one year, on the porch talking to someone who looked very familiar. As he walked closer, he gasped. It was Punatii!

2

She was a princess, a real Indian princess. The third child of the Maharaja of Bhabar, Punatii was no different from any other young girl. She had her dreams and aspirations. But most of all, she wanted to fall in love with the right man and live a life filled with happiness, loved by her family and friends.

Her father wanted his children to become "Westernized"— to learn the language, culture, and traditions of the Western world so they could more readily adapt to the changing world order. He especially wanted his children to understand the British, who had colonized India and would always be a part of India's future. With this intent, the Maharaja encouraged Punatii to associate with British children her own age. Since the Maharaja's realm encompassed the Naini Tal District and his estate was only a mile from Naini Tal village, Punatii became close friends with Maggie, Jim's sister.

Jim could not recall when he'd first met Punatii, but when he was nine years old he enjoyed playing the same boyish pranks on her as he did on his sisters. At that time, Punatii looked no different from other girls her age—skinny frame, jet-black hair tied in pigtails, large brown eyes, a little shy and mysterious, and very uncoordinated. He found particular delight in scaring Punatii and Maggie with disgusting insects or reptiles. Often when they went for a swim in the lake near Jim's house, he would throw stones and other objects at them, just to see how close he could come without hitting them. Jim also enjoyed swimming underwater so they could not see him sneaking up to grab their ankles or feet and pull them under.

Once, when Jim pulled Punatii beneath the surface, her shrieks of terror caused him to laugh so hard he inhaled a large quantity of lake water. After coughing, gagging, and choking for several minutes in an attempt to regain his breath, he looked up to see Maggie and Punatii howling with laughter.

Jim's pranks and antics did not make a favorable impression on Punatii. In fact, she thought Jim was a brat whose only intent was to make her life miserable. Despite the torment, Punatii continued to frequent Jim's house because of her close association with Maggie.

When Punatii was ten years old, her father sent her away so she could receive a better education and study the Western culture. Jim had not seen Punatii since then, which did not cause him any particular concern. Nor did Punatii miss Jim. However, Punatii did continue to write to Maggie, and when she finally returned home from school, she decided to visit her old friend again.

As Jim drew nearer, he was caught off guard by Punatii's beauty. She still had long, raven-black hair and enchanting dark brown eyes, but now she also had a shapely figure, and her smile was warm and enticing. The long, royal blue, silk sari she was wearing enhanced the whole picture for him. He approached her almost mesmerized, until he heard her infectious laugh when she glanced at him.

"Jim," Maggie said, "you do remember Punatii, don't you?"

"Indeed!" Jim turned toward the girl. "You are the skinny little creature who used to come here to play with Maggie."

"Yes," replied Punatii. She was astonished to see the transformation Jim had made from a small, lanky boy to the tall, handsome young man standing before her. "I suppose you are the same boy who used to torment me?"

Jim laughed. "I apologize for that. It was just a terrible phase I was going through. I'm a changed person now, really! Maggie can vouch for that."

"Maggie has told me that you've grown up, but I'm not sure whether I should believe her." Punatii cocked her head slightly, gazing suspiciously at Jim.

Maggie excused herself to help prepare dinner, and Jim took Maggie's chair next to Punatii. For the next thirty minutes, Jim and Punatii became reacquainted by telling each other about the events in their lives over the past four years. Punatii agreed to have dinner with the Corbetts, following which Jim walked Punatii back to her estate.

For the next several months, Jim and Punatii were almost inseparable. Jim took her hunting with him on many occasions, thoroughly enjoying her company on the long walks through the forest. Jim had never felt this way before. Normally quiet, he found himself chattering incessantly with Punatii. It seemed they could talk and laugh for hours, and never realize what had happened to the time.

One day when they were returning home from a walk in the forest, Jim noticed a beautiful lavender orchid growing adjacent to the trail. He cut a cluster of flowers with his knife, and carefully placed it in Punatii's hair. As he looked into her eyes, he saw the same longing he was feeling. He held her close to him and gently kissed her lips. As he slowly pulled back, he noticed tears in Punatii's eyes. She said nothing, and they continued their way back home. When Jim returned home, he could hardly contain his excitement about being able to see Punatii again.

Three days later, after Jim had bathed, he sat at the table to eat breakfast with his family. He was dressed in a clean, crisp drill outfit, prepared to attend the Saturday morning marching and rifle drill ceremony held by his company each week. Mary was already dressed for market, wearing a light gray dress with a matching apron. Jim was in a good mood and was humming an Irish love ballad. Mary was frying some fresh chicken eggs. She stopped suddenly, looked at Jim with a puzzled expression, then glanced at Maggie. Maggie reached over and touched Jim's arm.

"Punatii is moving to Moradabad today."

"What?" Jim thought he had heard her wrong.

"Her father promised her to the maharaja there. She is to be his wife."

"No! How do you know this?" Jim sat up in disbelief.

"I was at the palace yesterday when she told me. She wanted me to. . . . "

"Good Lord!" Jim interrupted. "Has she gone yet?"

"She was supposed to leave at first light."

Jim quickly rose from his chair, knocking it over backward. "I must see her!"

"Jim, no!" Maggie insisted. "It's too late. You can't interfere. . . "

"Who says I can't?" Jim cried as he bolted out the door. His brothers and sisters remained silent, surprised at Jim's behavior. Maggie and Mary stared at the screen door. Finally, Mary looked over at Maggie.

"I didn't think he would react this way. He must really be fond of her."

"More so than you think," Maggie responded pensively. "And Punatii is really keen on him too."

"Oh dear, I was worried something like this would happen." Mary gathered up the dishes and placed them in the sink. "Please try to cheer him up when he returns. I need to get straight away to market."

Twenty minutes later, Jim arrived at the Maharaja's castle out of breath. He pounded on the large oak door of the castle. A servant, clad in white cloth, opened the door and appeared surprised to see Jim.

"Corbett Sahib. . . "

"Is Punatii about?" asked Jim with desperation in his voice.

"She departed almost two hours ago," the servant said, puzzled that Jim was unaware of Punatii's plans.

Jim turned and ran up the dirt road to the juncture where one fork leads to Moradabad. As he rounded the bend at great speed, he slipped on some loose gravel and fell, scraping his leg on the rocks and dirt.

"Damn!" he yelled as he quickly stood up. He brushed himself off and continued running as fast as he could. Twenty minutes later, when he could run no farther, he collapsed on the ground to catch his breath. His chest was heaving, and sweat was pouring from his body, saturating his clothes. As he searched the road beyond for any sign of Punatii's entourage, he realized the hopelessness of his situation.

"Why . . . ?" he shouted at the empty road leading to Moradabad. "Why didn't you tell me?"

He sat on the road, pulled his knees up to his chest, folded his arms over his knees, and rested his head on his arms. As he sat there in solitude, the realization struck him that he would be late for drill. He didn't care. But as much as he wanted to run away and never return, he knew he had to face up to his responsibilities.

Later that day after drill, tears streamed from Jim's eyes as Sarge's cane lashed his backside. Sarge knew the tears were not from the thrashing but from something else. Nevertheless, personal problems or not, Sarge had his duty to do. British justice. No compassion. No excuses.

Jim finished school when he was seventeen, and quit his part-time job at the general store in Naini Tal. Although he was treated well by the owner, working as a stock boy did not pay much. Nevertheless, Jim was able to contribute some of his earnings to the family coffers, just as his older brothers had done until they got married and had to support their own families.

Between schooling, chores, and working part-time at the store, Jim had still managed to hone his hunting skills during his free time. Unable to afford a decent rifle, he continued to rely on the old double-barreled muzzleloader shotgun his cousin had given to him when he was eight years old. Only one barrel was operable; the other one was lashed to it with brass wire. Prior to that, Jim had used a slingshot and bow and arrows for hunting. The slingshot was capable of bringing down birds, and he had eventually become proficient enough with the bow and arrows to bring down larger birds and deer. Sarge had loaned Jim a .450 Martini-Henry rifle during the winter months while school was out, but Jim had to return it upon resumption of school each April.

Following his formal schooling, Jim was able to secure a job at Mankapur, where he supervised Indian laborers who cut timber to be used as fuel for the Bengal and North-Western trains. A year and a half later, Jim was transferred to Mokameh Ghat, a material trans-shipment station for the railroad southeast of Naini Tal in Bengal. Jim's responsibility entailed supervising over three hundred Indian workers who loaded materials from rail cars on the north side of the Ganges River onto barges; the materials were then transported to the south shore of the river and loaded onto other rail cars. It was work suitable only for a domiciled person of Jim's social stature, someone considered expendable by British expatriate authorities.

However, this position suited Jim to a tee. Not only was the pay reasonably good, but the job also enabled him to learn other dialects with which he was unfamiliar. The native workers soon began to admire and respect Jim. Not one to stand back and bark orders, Jim pitched in to help his men do the actual loading and unloading. It was backbreaking work—sixteen hours a day, seven days a week—but Jim knew his men would work harder if he set the example. They did.

Once, when their pay was delayed for three months, not one of Jim's workers walked off the job. They were concerned and upset because they had bills to pay and families to feed, but they trusted Jim's promise that their pay would be coming. In the interim, Jim rationed out funds from his own savings to the most needy, and was able to keep the workload on schedule.

Jim was able to return home only a few times during the year, normally on holidays. During a Hindu religious holiday break in early 1894, he decided to buy a rifle. He had saved every rupee he could over the previous three years, allowing for money that he had sent home. So, with money in hand, he visited his old boss at the general store.

"Good morning, Mister Matthews," greeted Jim as he extended his hand. "I trust you are well!"

"Good heavens!" shouted the elderly man as he grabbed Jim's hand. "It is good to see you again. How's the job doing?"

"Very well. Hard work, though."

"I certainly do miss you. Business has been bustling from all the new settlers in Naini Tal, and I'm having a devil of a time keeping up with demand."

"I noticed all the new homes being built. What's bringing the people here?"

"Climate mostly. It's much cooler here in the foothills than to the south of us. The dreadful heat this past summer caused many of them to move up here."

Naini Tal had been a well-kept secret until the early 1840s. Nestled in the Himalayan foothills, it was simply paradise—surrounded by untamed piney forests, crystal lakes, and streams, and teeming with wildlife. British hunters had stumbled across it accidentally while pursuing game, and the word soon spread about its natural beauty and mild climate. Initially, British gentry had built summer homes around Naini Tal to escape the intolerable heat in the lowlands. Later it became the summer governmental headquarters for the United Provinces, that move bringing with it many administrative positions such as the postmaster job that Jim's father had received.

"What brings you to the store?" Matthews queried as he continued to stock a shelf with flour sacks. He had aged significantly since Jim last saw him, arthritis hampering his movements. His hair had turned from gray to white, and his wrinkled skin betrayed his age.

"Just to see how you were keeping, and to ask if you had any hunting rifles in stock."

"A new shipment has just arrived. Over there, behind the counter. Help yourself—I have to finish stocking these blasted shelves."

Jim walked briskly to the counter and peered behind it with great expectation. He wasn't disappointed. There were four brand-new rifles—two .450-400 double-barreled beauties, and two .450 Martini-Henry single-barreled rifles, the latter known for its vicious kick and deadly accuracy. Jim picked up one of the double-barreled rifles, admiring its craftsmanship. He grabbed the dangling price tag and read the amount.

"Glory! I had no idea these cost so much."

Overhearing Jim, Matthews remarked, "Yes, they've really gone up a tidy sum the past couple of years. Same with the Martini-Henrys. Too much demand chasing limited supplies, I suppose."

Matthews saw the look of despair in Jim's eyes. "Would a twenty percent discount help, Jim?"

"I appreciate your generosity, Mister Matthews, but I am still short—far short."

"How much do you have?" Matthews asked as he walked up to Jim.

"Only two hundred rupees."

Matthews rubbed his whiskered chin while pondering Jim's dilemma.

"Tell you what, Lad. I'll sell you my old double-barrel for that amount." Matthews knew he could get considerably more for it, but he wanted to help Jim. "Don't go away—I'll be back straight away." Matthews limped through the torn gray curtains which served as a door separating the store from his living quarters, and disappeared momentarily. He returned carrying a worn but well-maintained .450-400. The stock and barrel were gleaming from a thin coat of oil, and the hammer and trigger mechanisms worked as though they were still new.

"Kept it in pretty good shape," Matthews reflected as Jim inspected the rifle. "Never used it much. Never had the time."

"Are you sure that's all you want for this?" Jim knew the rifle was worth much more.

"Consider it a gift," laughed Matthews. "I know you'll treat it well, and you'll get a lot more use out of it than I will."

"This really is a gift," exclaimed Jim. "Thanks! Every time I take it hunting, I'll bring you back some game, provided my aim is true."

"I'd like that!" chuckled Matthews. "Here are some cartridges for it. They are included in the price. And incidentally, I'll trade ammo for any fresh game you bring me. Now, why don't you take it to the forest and try it out?"

Jim gave Matthews the money and headed for the door, anxious to use his new rifle. "Thank you again, Mister Matthews! I very much appreciate your generosity."

Matthews smiled. "And by the way, how's your mother?"

"Busy as ever," Jim replied, "but keeping well." He swung the screen door open, took his leave of Matthews, and continued on his way.

As he watched Jim depart, Matthews returned to his task. "This damned store!" he muttered.

**3**

Jim practiced with his rifle until it became an extension of his being. He took it with him whenever he went in the forest—not only to hunt game but for protection. There had been more frequent reports of man-eating tigers and leopards during the previous two years, and Jim felt safe with his rifle by his side.

Man-eaters were a freak of nature, and young Jim had difficulty understanding why these large predators, which appeared so adept at hunting prey, would attack humans for food. Maybe they were injured or old. Certainly, there must be some logical explanation of why these great cats, which are by nature wary of man, altered their diet to include humans.

Jim had heard of entire villages terrorized by a man-eater. He could only imagine the people's fright. Afraid to leave their houses day or night for fear of being attacked, they eventually were driven to acts of desperation in order to obtain food and firewood. Then, when they were forced to leave their huts, the man-eater would be waiting.

Shivers tracked electrically up Jim's spine as he wondered what it must be like to be attacked by a tiger or leopard. Long, sharp fangs sinking into your neck, suffocating the life from your body, while razor-sharp claws lacerate your flesh to keep you from escaping. *Good Lord,* Jim thought, *if it ever happens to me, I hope death comes quickly.*

Three days before Jim was required to return to his job in Bengal, he overheard two of his Indian neighbors talking about a tiger they had seen in the forest nearby. Jim went over to inquire.

"Yes, Sahib," one of the Indians exclaimed, "we saw it crossing the trail near Downing's Rock."

Downing's Rock was named after a former British hunter, Miles Downing. Several years earlier, he was perched on top of the eight-foot-high boulder, waiting to ambush a large male tiger known to be in the area. He and his Indian servant had climbed up the backside of the rock, and he had assumed the prone position with his rifle near the edge facing the trail. His servant was sitting behind him, off to one side.

Apparently, as told by the hysterical servant following the incident, while they waited for the tiger to appear on the trail, the animal crept up behind Downing on the rock. The servant, who saw the tiger approaching, went into shock and could not move or make a sound. The tiger crept closer to the hunter and sniffed his feet. The hunter, believing his servant was making the noise, beckoned with his hand to be quiet while keeping his eyes trained on the trail to his front. The tiger, taking the hand-waving as a sign of aggression, growled threateningly. Upon hearing the growl, the hunter spun his head around to see a 450-pound tiger staring him in the face.

In his fright, the hunter fell off the boulder and landed on the hardened dirt trail, his scream ending as his neck was broken. The startled tiger bounded off into the forest, never to be seen in those parts again. The unfortunate servant never fully recovered from the ordeal, and never set foot in the forest again.

After Jim extracted all the particulars about the tiger from the two men, he ran home, grabbed his rifle and ammunition, and set off for Downing's Rock. When he arrived an hour later, he immediately put his hunting skills into action. First, he stood silently and listened to the forest. Assured that everything was normal, he walked up and down the trail, searching for pug marks. Approximately forty feet up the trail from the rock, another game trail crossed the main trail that he was on. It was at this crossing that he noticed the tiger's tracks. He analyzed the pug impressions carefully, noting some which were fresh. He followed the freshest marks to a nearby pool and found water seeping into one of the pug impressions.

*Glory!* Jim thought. *She must have passed through here only minutes ago.*

Jim knew it was a tigress by the distinctively narrow pug marks. He estimated her to be fully grown and of average weight—around 350 pounds.

This was an opportunity few hunters get. Jim's heart was pounding in anticipation of the hunt. Since it had rained during the preceding night, tracking would be easier. Not only would the pug marks be more prevalent, but the ground was still saturated enough to muffle his footsteps over leaves and twigs. Jim removed his leather boots and quietly donned the rubber slippers he had purchased recently for stalking game. He placed his boots under a protruding rock ledge, where they would remain dry and be hidden from the view of anyone walking along the trail.

Jim had to exercise the utmost caution during this hunt. There were no drag lines next to the cat's pug marks to indicate she was carrying recently killed prey. It was still possible the tigress had a kill in her mouth and it was too small to drag alongside her on the ground. Nevertheless, since no drag signs were visible, Jim was taught to assume the tigress had no prey.

He had little difficulty following the fresh, deep imprints in the soft earth. When the tigress traveled over gravel, rock, or through streams, Jim easily picked up her trail where the soft ground resumed. The tigress proceeded on a fairly straight course and at a constant speed, indicating that she was in no hurry and was not alarmed.

As Kunwah had taught him years before, Jim stopped frequently to listen to the sounds of the forest. Occasionally, he heard the alarm call of peafowl or langur monkeys to his front. This reassured him the tigress was still on course and allowed him to gauge the distance between him and his quarry.

The piney fragrance from the evergreens and sweet aroma from the rhododendron flowers along the trail heightened Jim's senses. Sunlight poured into breaks in the forest where the tree canopy opened to the heavens. The tigress kept to the forest's shadows, masking her movements. When Jim ascended a forested hill to the top, he looked down at the pug marks once again.

*Bloodstains!* he acknowledged excitedly. *And scratches in the dirt where the tigress repositioned her hold on her kill!*

Jim was ecstatic. Knowing the tigress was carrying a kill meant she would be searching for a safe place to eat her prey. Just then, the tigress growled. Jim flattened himself to the ground. His heart beat faster; shivers were racing from his spine to the nape of his neck.

*Go easy!* he commanded himself. *Now is not the time to panic.* When he regained control of his screaming nerves, he thought of Kunwah. Then he listened intently while remaining preternaturally silent. Seconds later, Jim heard the distinct clatter of dislodged stones coming from the bottom of the hill. This was followed by a chuffing noise made by the tigress.

Jim peered at the area from which he believed the noises originated, but saw nothing. His panic swelled as he wondered if the tigress knew of his presence and was coming to investigate. He heard her growl again, and noticed a thick cluster of brush agitating directly below him and to his front. The tigress had selected a good location in which to eat her meal. The brush provided her excellent concealment, so Jim had no choice but to wait until she revealed herself.

Minutes passed endlessly while Jim continued listening to the tigress crunching bone and cartilage, interspersed with angry growls apparently caused by an occasional uncooperative morsel. Finally, serene silence pervaded the area. Even the birds stopped chirping. Anticipation swelled in Jim.

*Come on! Come out into the open!* his mind seemed to scream.

An eerie, guttural resonance emanated from the brush, followed by the faint rustle of leaves. A slippery, sweaty finger wrapped itself around the trigger, hoping for that brief split-second of opportunity. Perspiration beaded Jim's forehead, and his heart began to hammer relentlessly. Jim went rigid.

Suddenly, a fiery orange-and-white apparition appeared directly in front of the bushes—thirty feet from Jim. Its muzzle was stained red with blood, and it gazed intently at Jim. Feeling threatened, it sent a thick, menacing snarl reverberating off the surrounding hillsides. It skinned its lips back from its four-inch ivory fangs, then hissed a bloodcurdling sound that could mean only one thing: The enraged tigress was going to charge.

The tone of its savage fury was daunting. Jim felt prickling at the nape of his neck—iciness in his gut. A shiver rippled through him as he held his aim on the tigress's chest, just below her lower jaw.

Jim saw ears lay back and jaws open wide as he squeezed the trigger. The sound was deafening. The tigress, feeling the heavy lead bullet penetrate deep inside her chest, reared back on her haunches and fell over backward. She scrambled to regain her footing and bounded up the hill opposite Jim. Halfway up the hill, she fell onto her side. Her breathing was harsh and sporadic for several seconds. She thrashed wildly at the air with her right front paw, claws extended. Then suddenly, her breathing stopped and she lay still.

Jim was shocked into a trance. He watched the tigress's reaction to his shot, but felt he was somewhere far away, seeing the scene through a powerful telescope. When reality finally returned, he rammed another cartridge into the empty chamber. He walked closer to the tigress, picked up three stones, and pelted the carcass.

Convinced the big cat was dead, Jim cautiously approached the carcass to inspect his prize. She was healthy and full-grown, approximately five years old. Her coat was bright orange with vivid jet-black stripes. Jim was overtaken by its beauty.

Although he felt a twinge of remorse for destroying such an awesome creature, he was overjoyed that this feat thrust him into manhood. Although he had successfully hunted leopards in the past, this was his first tiger. Hunting was "king" in India, and the ultimate prize for any hunter was to bag a tiger. In an age when deeds defined a man, killing one of nature's most fearsome predators won the hunter the rite of passage.

No longer would Jim have to listen to other hunters tell their stories of successful tiger hunts. No longer would he have to envy other big-game hunters and long to be as good as they were. He was now numbered among them. He could now tell his hair-raising story of how he stalked and shot nature's largest and most dangerous and elusive predatory cat—the tiger.

Jim reveled in his glory for several minutes, then removed his hunting knife from the sheath and began to skin the tigress. Vultures and magpies crowded onto tree branches to watch the process. Their raucous cries were a vain attempt to hurry Jim to finish his chore so they could begin their feast.

Jim took his time. Although he was adept at skinning animals, this was his first tiger. He wanted to make sure the job was done right. There would be no second try. An hour later, Jim severed the last paw from the leg, leaving the skin intact, and carefully rolled the pelt into a ball. He placed the pelt into a jute mesh bag carried for such purposes, and stepped away from the carcass. The swarming, bloodthirsty flies were tormenting him as much as they were the carcass.

As Jim hoisted the forty-pound jute bag over his shoulder to begin his two-mile journey back to Naini Tal, the vultures descended en masse onto the remains. Jim marveled at how they served a definite purpose in cleaning up carrion.

When Jim arrived at Naini Tal, he did not go directly home. His first destination was O'Malley's pub, where he could proudly display his trophy. As he pushed open the swinging cafe doors, he spotted his friend Kyle sitting at the bar. There were some thirty men in the pub, most of whom Jim knew, the few strangers either passing travelers or recent visitors to Naini Tal on vacation or to hunt.

Jim placed his rifle against the wall near the door and walked over to his friend. Kyle, engaged in a heated conversation with two other boisterous men, looked up to see Jim approaching.

"What's in the bag, Jim?"

Jim remained silent as he pulled the pelt out and unrolled it on the dusty wooden floor.

"A tiger!" Kyle exclaimed.

A murmur of voices erupted as the others crowded around the pelt to get a better look and to touch it.

"Now, where did you steal the pelt, laddie?" the big Irishman sitting next to Kyle blurted out as he slicked back his thinning hair with his massive hand. His nose and face were as red as his cotton shirt, no doubt attributable to the quantity of alcohol he had consumed. When he belched, the odor verified Jim's suspicions.

"Picked up its tracks near Downing's Rock," Jim explained in earnest. "Followed it for a few hundred yards northwest until I came across it feeding on its kill in some thick bush."

*"Harrr,"* the Irishman laughed as he slapped his knee. "That's what you'd like us to believe, right, laddie?"

"If Jim says that's how it happened, that's how it happened," Kyle interrupted. "I've never known Jim to tell tales about something like this."

"Well, I think you're both a pair of liars," bellowed the Irishman, hawking up a huge gob of phlegm and spitting it onto the prostrated pelt.

Jim stared at the disgusting sight, not knowing what to say or do next. Kyle knew. Instinctively, he sent his fist smashing into the Irishman's face, the force of the punch knocking the burly drunk off his stool and onto the dusty floor.

"Now we're in it," said Jim.

The ensuing brawl was similar to an old western knock-down-drag-out bar fight. It happened often at O'Malley's. First, an argument—normally over something insignificant; then, a punch.

The first punch was always the catalyst that ignited the room into a frenzied free-for-all. When it was over, everyone went home with cuts and bruises. No one ever got seriously hurt. Everyone was too soused with alcohol to inflict any lasting damage.

This was the menfolk's idea of a good time in Naini Tal. Following the donnybrook, everyone went home singing arm-in-arm, more for support than camaraderie, leaving O'Malley to clean up the mess. But O'Malley was used to it. That's why he nailed the few tables in his pub to the floor and had heavy, thick oak chairs to sit on. This minimized the damage, and cleaning up was a simple chore. Besides, he liked to mix it up with the men on occasion too, just to hone his fighting edge.

An hour later, Jim and Kyle pushed through the screen door at Jim's house. Jim was supporting his buddy by holding onto Kyle's left arm, which was wrapped around Jim's neck. Jim's right arm was circled around Kyle's waist. The two stunk of rum and were in no pain irrespective of their bloodied faces. They were singing an old Irish love ballad off-key, slurring the words and laughing in their stupor.

"Oh, no," cried Maggie as she watched them enter. "Not again!" She grabbed the bandages and antiseptic from the cupboard and helped Jim place Kyle into a chair. "What happened this time?"

"No worries, Sis," Jim laughed. "Kyle and I had a minor disagreement with some fool over a tiger, and we had to flatten 'im."

"Yeassh," slurred Kyle. "He will not quickly forget ush!"

"From the looks of your faces, you two won't be forgetting him either." Maggie dabbed some antiseptic on Kyle's facial cuts while Jim went back outside to get the tiger pelt he had placed on the porch before they'd entered.

"Did I ever tell you how lovely you are?" Kyle asked while gazing into Maggie's face with bloodshot eyes and trying to keep his balance on the chair.

"Only when you're potted. You never have the nerve when you're sober, Love." Maggie and Kyle enjoyed teasing each other with amorous witticisms. They both knew not to take each other seriously. Maggie was plain like her mother and was socially incapable of attracting any suitors. She was extremely shy around men and avoided engaging in conversations with them. "I don't have time for suitors," she had always told Mary when the subject arose. "Anyway, Jim needs so much looking after." That usually ended the subject.

Kyle regarded Maggie as a sister. He had spent so much time with her and Jim when they were growing up, it was difficult for Kyle to consider Maggie as anything but kin.

Besides, everyone knew that Kyle had a crush on Beth Jamison, who lived three houses down from him. And anyone who knew Beth knew she felt the same about Kyle.

"Sis, take a look at this!" Jim uncoiled the pelt on the floor. Maggie gasped in disbelief. Kyle keeled over in the chair and landed on the floor with a loud thud. He had passed out.

Maggie's surprise turned to disgust. "You two are pathetic."

4

At age twenty-seven, Jim's reputation as a big-game hunter was renowned throughout the district. So it was no surprise to him when District Deputy Commissioner Berthoud asked Jim to take his visiting niece on a hunting expedition. Sarah Mendelson, Berthoud's niece, was twenty-one years of age with slender build, reddish hair, dazzling blue eyes, and a face full of freckles that seemed to dance in the sunlight.

Her father, a wealthy businessman in London, had suggested that Sarah visit her favorite uncle in India while the country was still under British rule. Sarah jumped at the opportunity. She had read numerous stories about "wild" India, and especially enjoyed Rudyard Kipling's *Jungle Book*. A tomboy at heart, Sarah dreamed of traveling to India and being able to see firsthand the tigers, leopards, and elephants she had read about.

When Jim was introduced to Sarah at the district deputy commissioner's residence, he felt a definite attraction to her. It had been a long time since Jim had let his guard down to those feelings. After Punatii was sent off to the Maharaja of Moradabad, he swore he'd never look at another girl. When Sarah smiled at him and shyly shook his hand, however, Jim's vow suddenly became a distant memory.

"Hello," Sarah said softly. "My uncle told me you have quite a reputation for hunting large game."

Jim blushed just a bit, but it felt good. "I'm not sure what you've heard about me, but it was probably exaggerated," he said, removing his hat.

Sarah giggled. "I'm sure you're modest about your achievements. I'm Sarah." She extended her hand.

Jim laughed as he shook her hand gently. "I understand you'll be joining us tomorrow to hunt pheasant," he said, holding it a bit longer than necessary.

"Yes. Do you object?"

"Not at all. My sister, Maggie, will be coming with us to help keep you company. She often goes with me and has even bested me on several occasions."

"How marvelous! I can't tell you how much I've been looking forward to this."

Jim's face beamed. "Splendid! See you at first light."

Jim's feet never touched the ground as he walked home that evening. He could not get that beautiful enchantress he had just met off his mind. He was certainly looking forward to the hunt on the following day, if only for the opportunity to see Sarah again.

The next morning's hunting party consisted of Jim, Maggie, Deputy Commissioner Berthoud and his wife, Julia, and Sarah. Not only was the weather absolutely gorgeous, but they had incredible luck. They shot fifteen pheasants, and decided to serve them at a welcoming party for Sarah that her uncle and aunt were hosting on the following day.

Later that night, Jim decided to question Maggie about Sarah. He beat around the bush for several minutes, then finally decided to be blunt.

"Would you find out how she feels about me?"

"Oh, Jim," Maggie admonished, "you sound like a schoolboy asking his friend to find out if a certain girl is keen on him. Why don't you ask her to go on one of your excursions in the forest?"

Jim lowered his head sheepishly. "All right, then," he said. "I was just hoping she might have said something to you when we were hunting today."

Maggie laughed. "I'm entrusted with Sarah's confidence, and I cannot reveal anything she told me in secret. However, if you must know, she thinks you are ruggedly handsome. I told her she had been in the sun too long!"

"Thanks, Maggie!" Jim said facetiously. "I hope I can return the compliment one day."

"Oh, don't be so thin-skinned! I think Sarah is delightful. I'm not going to interfere, though. You're on your own, dear brother."

"I always appreciate your candid remarks, dear sister." Jim kissed Maggie on the forehead, then walked to the front porch with a big smile on his face.

Maggie watched Jim depart with a concerned look on her face. She often wondered if she and her mother would be able to make ends meet without Jim's financial help. Her other brothers either had left India or were supporting families of their own. If Jim ever married, he would need every rupee he could muster to take care of his own family. Not that Jim would purposely ignore his mother's and Maggie's financial needs, but the meager pay in India went only so far.

During the party, Jim offered to take Sarah on an excursion through the forest to search for orchids, and she readily accepted. Jim could not hide his nervousness when he met Sarah the following morning at her residence, but his anxiety quickly subsided when they reached the forest. Here, Jim was in his element. He easily pointed out and correctly identified many flora that grew native in the area. Sarah was impressed with Jim's extensive knowledge of botany. Her inquisitiveness was a joy to Jim, giving him the opportunity to share his knowledge with someone he truly cared about.

Following a picnic lunch that Sarah had brought along, they walked to a special place where Jim knew they would find an abundance of beautiful orchids. It was located next to an open grassy glade with a small, clear stream running through it. Sarah, overjoyed with the bounty, was busy selecting a few orchids to take back home when Jim noticed something moving through the bushes near the glade below them. He cautioned Sarah to remain silent, and as the two directed their attention to the glade, a large tigress walked into the sunlight streaking through the surrounding trees. The tigress was still wearing her thick, bright orange-and-black winter coat. Sarah stared in disbelief.

"It's so beautiful!" she whispered. "I can't believe I'm actually seeing a tiger in the wild."

Jim smiled as he raised his rifle. "D'you fancy its pelt for a trophy?"

"No! Heavens, no! How could you think of shooting something so regal?" Sarah placed her hand on the barrel, pushing it down.

Jim was perplexed over Sarah's conservationist attitude. "India has over thirty thousand tigers," he whispered. "One less won't upset the balance of nature. Besides, some of the villages in the foothills are becoming more threatened by tigers. There's been increasing reports of attacks, and a man-eating tigress has already killed over fifty people near Champawat village."

"I just couldn't stand to see such a beautiful creature destroyed," pleaded Sarah. "Jim, please don't shoot it."

Jim slowly laid his rifle on the ground as the tigress disappeared from sight on the far side of the glen. He was surprised that Sarah had such a strong love of nature, and what he considered a Hindu "live-and-let-live" philosophy concerning all living things. He had grown up in a savage land. It was kill or be killed. Men in this part of the country were noted for their hunting prowess. To take the life of a tiger, leopard, or other large animal was proof of one's mettle. The number of tiger and leopard pelts you possessed was related directly to your courage, and won the respect and admiration of your peers.

"I'm sorry, Jim," Sarah continued, "but I cannot condone killing these majestic animals. I believe God put them on this earth for our pleasure and for food, and to live in harmony with us. What would happen if man continued to destroy tigers until there were none left for future generations to enjoy? What a sad and tragic world this would be. How can mankind possibly re-create an animal species he thoughtlessly eradicated from the earth?"

Jim pondered Sarah's words carefully. "I never thought that we would ever be able to do such a thing. As long as I can remember, there has always been an abundance of tigers in India." Jim scratched his head. "I don't think shooting them in sport has caused any large decline in their numbers. When one is killed, another tiger soon moves into the territory. Does your 'do-not-kill' philosophy also apply to tigers and leopards that turn into man-eaters?"

"Don't be absurd! Animals that kill humans are a queer phenomenon and must be destroyed. My philosophy applies only to animals that cause us no harm. By the way, why do you think that tiger near Champawat turned into a man-eater?"

"I don't know. Maybe it cannot catch its normal prey because of injury or old age. You may not believe me, Sarah, but I do worry about the tiger's plight in India. Every time I visit villages throughout the Kumaon Hills, I discover that more forested land has been converted to agricultural use through slash-and-burn methods. At the current rate, maybe fifty or sixty years from now there may not be sufficient forested land for India's larger wildlife to survive. I believe it will be the growing human population that will cause the demise of tigers and leopards, not the rifle."

Sarah sighed. "Perhaps you're right, Jim." She leaned over and kissed him on the cheek. "Thanks for sparing the tiger's life. Maybe if my uncle talks to the right people, something could be done to prevent the destruction of India's wildlife." Sarah smiled. "I am so happy that I was able to actually see a tiger in the wild. Future generations may never have that opportunity."

Jim caressed Sarah's cheek with his fingers, placed his hand in hers, and they slowly walked home with her head leaning on Jim's shoulder. Jim never felt closer to another human being in all his life.

During the next three months, whenever Jim could take time off from work, he and Sarah continued to enjoy each other's company. Sarah was in Jim's thoughts constantly, and even he was amazed at the effect she was having on him. Although he could not put it in words, she made Jim a better person than he knew himself to be. Each day, Jim awoke with a joyous feeling about life, knowing he was going to be with Sarah. He shared his feelings with Sarah, but she remained silent, although he sensed she felt the same about him. Finally, one day Jim garnered enough courage to propose marriage, and decided to tell Maggie first.

"I think you're rushing into this too quickly," Maggie cautioned. "Sarah's not like us, Jim. She has led a pampered life in England."

"I don't care, Maggie," he mumbled excitedly. "I'm going straight away to ask her now."

Maggie tried her best to look cheerful when she bid Jim good luck as he left for the deputy commissioner's house. When he arrived at the residence, he found the commissioner's wife sitting on the porch.

"Good morning, Missus Berthoud. Is Sarah about?"

"No, she isn't, Jim. Her uncle took her to the railway station this morning. She's returning to London. Here, she wanted me to give you this." Julia handed Jim a letter addressed to him in Sarah's handwriting.

"London!" Jim looked surprised. "Why didn't she tell me? What happened?"

"I think everything will be explained in the letter, Jim," Julia stammered. "You'd better sit down."

Jim could sense that Julia was withholding something from him. When he unfolded the letter, his thoughts turned to Punatii.

My dearest Jim,

By the time you read this letter, I'll be on my way to London. Although my heart fervently disagrees with my decision to leave, I hope someday you will forgive me and realize this is best for both of us.

Last year I was diagnosed with terminal leukemia. My doctor didn't know for certain how much longer I would live, but indicated my chances were slim that I would survive another year. I am much too fond of you to let you see me suffer during my final days. I feel like a mortally wounded animal that only wants to crawl away to some remote cave and spend its remaining living moments in peace.

What we shared together I will treasure always. I sincerely hope you find the right woman someday who can grow old with you and share your love and passion for life. Please do not be upset with my uncle and aunt. I made them promise not to tell anyone of my condition.

I wish you all the happiness in the world.

Affectionately,


(signed) Sarah


Jim was stunned. He felt a terrible hollowness inside his chest. It was as though someone had ripped his heart out. When he regained his composure, he slowly stood up and returned home. On his way back, he looked toward the bright blue sky and cried mournfully, "Why? Oh, for God's sake, why?"

Five months later, Jim received a wire informing him of Sarah's death.

5

Dharva, along with twenty other women from Pali village, had walked nearly a half-mile to a stand of oak trees to cut leafy branches as fodder for their cattle. It was sunny and bright, and the air had just been cleansed by a monsoon rain shower.

En route to the remote area, the women had been chattering about the many things of importance in their lives, including their husbands, boyfriends, children, food, and life in general. However, the main topic revolved around the man-eating tiger, which had taken so many lives throughout the past four years.

They all knew of someone, family member or friend, who had fallen victim to the tiger, so they were understandably nervous about venturing so far from the village. Nevertheless, it was the women's duty to care for the livestock and ensure their cattle had ample fodder to eat.

When the women arrived at the cluster of oak trees, they all selected a tree in which to climb and lop off branches. Dharva and two of her friends selected a large tree located in a shallow ravine. They climbed into the tree and began chopping away at the branches with their sickles. As they went about their work, they continued talking and laughing.

Dharva, deciding that she had cut enough branches, informed her two friends that she was going to climb down and gather the branches together. While one of the women acknowledged Dharva's decision, the other woman became distracted by a gray langur monkey chattering its alarm in a tree farther down into the ravine.

"Dharva!" she exclaimed. "Do you hear the monkey? Something has upset it."

Dharva turned toward the langur and watched it scamper back and forth on a large branch while calling its alarm. She then looked down into the ravine to see if anything there was alarming the monkey.

"I do not see anything," she replied to her friend. "I do not know what has frightened the monkey."

"Something has, for certain," her friend responded. "If you climb down, be careful!"

Looking around the area again and seeing nothing amiss, Dharva started her slow descent. Simultaneously, a tigress crept out from behind a large rock into the open with its belly touching the ground. It glanced at the other women momentarily and, assured it had not been detected, took several more quick steps toward the oak tree.

The langur continued its alarm calls, but the women paid it no heed. When Dharva was eight feet from the ground, the tigress sprang from its position, bounded to the tree, stood on its hind legs, and clamped its massive jaws around Dharva's foot.

"*AIIEEE!*" Dharva screamed, feeling the horrible pain surging through her body to her brain. Her cry jolted the other women, who gasped collectively when they saw the tigress pulling on Dharva's foot.

The tigress grunted loudly as it tugged relentlessly at its prey. Dharva continued to cry out in anguish, desperately clinging to a branch and hoping the tiger would release its grip. However, Dharva's strength was no match for the tigress's power. Using its muscular forelegs, it pushed away from the tree trunk. Skin ripped from Dharva's hands and fingers as she succumbed to the tigress's weight and strength.

As the woman fell to the ground, the tigress quickly grasped her by the neck and ran back into the ravine. The other women watched the terrifying scene without uttering a sound. They were shocked into silence. Several minutes after they had watched the tigress drag Dharva's lifeless body into a thicket some two hundred yards away, they climbed down from the trees and ran back to the village, fearing for their own lives. When they arrived at the village, they immediately thanked the gods that it was Dharva's turn to die and not theirs.

"Surely Dharva must have done something to offend the gods," one woman lamented. "Otherwise, the tiger would not have taken her." The other women agreed.

Meanwhile, Jim had just returned to Naini Tal on vacation from his job in Bengal, and decided to attend a conference being held at the town hall. The purpose of the meeting was to discuss the situation concerning the man-eating tigress near Champawat village. The tigress had been driven out of Nepal by enraged villagers over four years earlier, after it had killed two hundred people there. Since its arrival in India, the beast had added another two hundred souls to its list of victims.

This was the first reported man-eater of such significance in the United Provinces. Other humans had been attacked and killed by tigers and leopards throughout the provinces, but most were sporadic incidents. Predators that had killed more than three humans were officially classified as man-eaters, and the British government instigated measures to put each killer out of business. Normally, a bounty was placed on the animal. This monetary reward, plus the distinction of destroying a man-eater were often sufficient enticement to attract big-game hunters to test their luck and skill.

Despite the four-hundred-rupee bounty placed on the Champawat man-eater and the numerous attempts by famous hunters to destroy her, she still was able to elude death and remained at large. Her territory covered over two hundred square miles of the most treacherous terrain in northern India, consisting of heavily forested hills, deep ravines, numerous rivers, thick undergrowth, and many areas containing acres of large boulders. She had lived in this area for more than four years and was familiar with every avenue of escape and places in which to hide from her pursuers. She had picked her territory well. It was heavily populated, and the numerous small villages provided her an ample supply of food—humans!

Since the tigress had turned man-eater, she had quickly overcome her fear of man. She had learned that humans were easy prey that satisfied her insatiable hunger for meat. She also learned to stalk her human prey during daylight as well as darkness. Like most animals, these humans were predictable in their routines. They normally traveled the same routes through the forest, cut wood in the same places, tended their crops and livestock in the same places, and went to market in the same places. It was so easy, at first.

However, during the past two years it had become more difficult for her to find human prey. They remained closer to their villages and did not travel through the forest as frequently. When they did move about, they traveled in large groups and made loud noises to frighten the tigress away. But the hungry tigress had learned to overcome these obstacles. She had learned that attacking someone in a group caused the rest to scatter and run away. She also became bolder in other ways, attacking people within the village boundaries, often close to their homes.

It was this new boldness and relentless killing that caused a state of panic among the villagers and Indian authorities. They demanded the British government do something to destroy the man-eater immediately. It was the British who had the most modern rifles, and to whom the Indian natives looked for protection.

It was at this conference in Naini Tal that the most capable and prominent people in the provinces gathered to discuss any and all options available to rid the countryside of this menace. Indian officials and royalty attended from the surrounding areas. British government officials were present from Delhi, as well as from the districts within the provincial boundary. The lieutenant governor of the United Provinces, Sir John Hewett, presided over the conference and solicited all advice possible from the attendees.

One person suggested forming a massive "beat" to drive the tigress into Nepal. That idea was quickly rejected. Not only was the lieutenant governor reluctant to offend his neighbors in Nepal, but there would be no guarantee the tigress would not return to the Champawat area following the beat. Another person suggested building several outposts in places the tigress normally visited and staffing them with sharpshooters and sufficient food and supplies to last several weeks. The idea had merit, but Hewett discounted it after realizing the tigress was not a slave to routine and thus was not predictable.

Finally, after listening to all the comments concerning the tiger's behavior and suggestions for remedial action, Hewett signaled the throng to be silent while he presented his deliberation.

"First of all, I want to express my gratitude for your attendance here today. I truly sympathize with the plight of all the villagers living under the tyranny of this menace, and applaud your efforts to put an end to the man-eater's reign of terror.

"I am aware of earlier attempts to destroy this wretched beast, and have considered all the proposals brought forth today. From what we know about the tiger, it is in the prime of life and will continue to kill humans for many more years unless we can put an end to it.

"Obviously, placing a bounty on the tiger has not worked. It has resulted in attracting too many hunters to the area, which has caused great confusion and destruction. Over the past three years, since the bounty has been in effect, three hunters were shot by other hunters, and many innocent tigers, bears, leopards, deer, and livestock have been killed by hunters who thought they were shooting at the man-eater.

"In retrospect, I believe our best hope of destroying the killer is to restrict the area to only one hunter who is willing to track the tiger for as long as it takes to destroy it."

There erupted a concerted murmuring of disapproval and conjecture over Hewett's proposal. Most of those in attendance were of the opinion that no one person would be willing or able to undertake such a venture. To hunt an established man-eater alone in a highly treacherous territory exceeding two hundred square miles would be suicidal.

When the crowd quieted down, Hewett asked, "Do we have such a volunteer present?" For the next minute, the murmuring continued to increase in volume while everyone looked around the room to see if anyone would be willing to risk the endeavor. No one volunteered.

"Well," Hewett continued, obviously exasperated that no one was willing to undertake the task, "if there are no volunteers, this meeting is adjourned. Nevertheless, the offer remains in effect until someone can convince me of a better solution. Thank you for coming!"

Jim thought about volunteering, but did not want to do it in front of a large assembly. Although he was unfamiliar with destroying man-eaters, he felt confident he would have as much success as any other hunter. As Jim and Maggie filed out the door and headed for home, Deputy District Commissioner Berthoud grabbed Jim by his shirtsleeve.

"Mister Corbett," he said softly, "can I speak to you for a moment?"

Surprised, Jim answered, "Of course!"

Berthoud continued, "The governor and I are quite desperate to find someone willing to tackle this mission. I know that you're one of the best big-game hunters in the district, and was hoping I could talk you into trying your luck with the man-eater."

Jim was speechless and did not know how to answer.

"These are your people who are being attacked and killed by this beast," Berthoud proclaimed. "Don't you feel compelled to help them?"

This was a low blow, but Berthoud wanted to appeal to Jim's status as domiciled, knowing Jim felt a greater kinship to the natives than the expatriates did. It had the desired effect.

"All right," said Jim, angered and challenged by Berthoud's remark.

"No, Jim!" Maggie whispered loudly as she grabbed his arm. "Are you *mental?*" Just then, she realized her mistake. If Jim backed out now, it would be an affront to his pride. *Curse the wretched creature!* she said to herself.

"Splendid!" said Berthoud as he lit up like a Christmas tree. "What can I do to help? What provisions will you need?"

Jim sighed. "I'll need funding for six porters, as well as provisions for a fortnight."

"Why only two weeks?" Berthoud asked.

"If I haven't destroyed the man-eater by then, my nerves will be so frazzled that I'll need a rest. Besides, I'll need to return to my job in Bengal."

Berthoud laughed. "I see. Anything else?"

"Yes. Rescind the bounty on the man-eater."

"Why?" Berthoud asked, perplexed.

Jim looked him straight in the eye. "I'm not a reward hunter."

Berthoud nodded. "I'll take care of it immediately. By the way, how soon can you leave for Champawat?"

"Provided everything falls into place, I should be able to depart within three days."

"Good!" replied Berthoud, obviously pleased with himself. "I'll inform the governor immediately. I know he'll be pleased."

Berthoud slapped Jim on the back, then turned and walked toward the governor's office.

"How could you?" Maggie exclaimed, tears in her eyes.

"Maggie, don't be upset. Nothing will happen to me. You know how careful I am."

Maggie looked into Jim's eyes, shook her head, then ran toward their house. Just then, Peter Dunford, a renowned hunter who had tried to kill the man-eater a year earlier, took Jim's arm. "I couldn't help but overhear your conversation with Berthoud. I think it's a courageous thing you're doing and want to wish you luck."

"Thanks," replied Jim, watching Maggie running away.

Peter continued. "Since you have not hunted man-eaters before, I would like to share my experiences with you. It might help."

"Of course. I would appreciate anything you can tell me."

The two began walking toward Jim's house. "Jim, the first thing you need to keep in mind is that man-eaters are unpredictable. You're used to hunting tigers that are afraid of humans. The tigers you've encountered in the past have tried to avoid you, or run away if you've come upon them by surprise. You have been able to walk through the forest and fear nothing. But now, when you're tracking this man-eater, you'll have to be aware of everything around you. This devil sees you as its next meal, and is not afraid of you.

"It could be hiding behind a boulder or clump of bushes next to the track, waiting to attack you as you walk by. That's how ol' Jerry Knowles died. Or, it could stalk you as you make your way through dense undergrowth, and sneak up behind you when the wind is blowing from your front. That's how Ben Thomas was killed. Ron Chiles got mauled when the tiger climbed up the back of the tree he was sitting in and attacked him from behind. Fortunately, Ron fell from the tree before the tiger had a secure hold on him, and he was able to get away.

"What I'm trying to say, not to put too fine a point on it, is to always expect the unexpected. Hunting man-eaters requires a whole new dimension to what you already know. It requires you to use and rely on all your senses, and then some!"

"Thanks. What specifically can you tell me about this tiger?"

"Not much. Only saw it twice, and both times it was in limited light. It appeared to be large—I'd guess about four hundred pounds. Couldn't tell if it had any injury. It walks and runs like any normal tiger. But, the spooky thing about this one is the way it differentiates hunters from unprotected villagers. It has a knack of eluding anyone with a rifle.

"Another thing—the tiger seems to appear out of nowhere, and can vanish just as fast! Like a ghost or phantom. You might spot it off in the distance, but before you can train your rifle on it, it disappears into thin air. The man-eater knows the territory better than anyone. When things get too hot for it in one area, it heads for another place. Unfortunately, there are enough villages and small enclaves of families scattered throughout the area where it'll always find humans to hunt.

"I was on the run constantly, going from village to village trying to track it down. It was always one step ahead of me. After four months of chasing shadows, I had to get out of there. My nerves were finished. Anyway, I wish you luck! I hope I've been of some help."

"Of course you have, ol' chap." Jim shook Peter's hand vigorously. "Thanks again!"

"Keep your eyes in the back of your head!" shouted Peter as Jim walked away and headed for home to prepare for his journey.

**6**

Maggie was conspicuously silent throughout the day while Jim was preparing for his hunt. Attempts to console her and allay her fears concerning his decision were in vain. Maggie knew the dangers inherent in hunting man-eaters. Many who had volunteered for the venture in the past were either dead or permanently disfigured due to mauling by the hunted beast. Some victims' remains were never recovered, presuming the man-eater had devoured their entire bodies as well as their blood-soaked clothing.

Man-eating tigers and leopards were a phenomenon that caused fear and speculation to run rampant among the British populace in India. British newcomers, hearing stories about their countrymen who fell victim to attack, were frightened enough over normal tigers. Now that nature had caused some of these animals to forgo their normal diet in favor of humans, it only added to their terror. Even more important was the devastating effect these man-eaters were having among the native population living in the Himalayan foothills, where the majority of the man-eaters took up residence. The toll of human lives taken by just one of these man-eaters, left unchecked, would become difficult to fathom.

Such was the case of the Champawat man-eater, which over the previous several years had accumulated a list of more than four hundred victims. Since its territory encompassed approximately two hundred square miles, almost every family living within its realm had suffered the loss of at least one member. As the number of victims increased, more pressure was placed on the British government for resolution.

Jim was pleasantly surprised at the number of local village men who wanted to accompany him on the hunt. He thought he would have a tough time persuading anyone to go along; however, he found ten men from whom to choose. Eliminating the married men, he pared the number down to six. They would carry his tent, equipment, and other supplies needed for the duration.

To compensate for the risky endeavor, he decided to offer three times the normal wages they could expect to receive during the two-week period. Jim paid them half in advance and promised the remaining half when they returned to Naini Tal. He told them that if anything happened to him, they could collect the remainder from Maggie.

Jim decided to take his horse, a young chestnut mare, along with him to ride when they were traveling over relatively flat terrain. Everything was assembled in a convenient manner, which would make their departure bright and early the next morning a quick and easy task. Jim caressed the highly accurate .450 Martini-Henry rifle and the .500 modified cordite rifle he'd selected to take along. He laid aside sufficient ammunition for the trip, then turned his attention to a more important matter—Maggie.

"I hope you understand why I volunteered to go," Jim said to her as he approached her on the porch.

"No, I don't," Maggie replied softly, "but I'm trying to. Is it Punatii or Sarah?"

"They might be part of the reason, but it's more than that. We have to live in these hills with these poor, unfortunate villagers. They look to us for help when they're troubled. When I journey through their villages, I can see the pleading in their eyes. Good Lord, Maggie, you don't see their hurt and suffering. I do, and I have to do something about it. I can't sit back any longer, hoping someone else will finally accomplish what I should have done years ago. Many lives have been lost due to my apathy, and my conscience won't allow me to continue ignoring the problem." Jim touched Maggie's arm softly. "Please understand!"

Maggie continued to rock in her chair, and thought about Jim's explanation carefully for several seconds without responding. Finally, she began to cry. "I'm sorry for being so selfish, Jim. It's just that I couldn't cope if anything happened to you." Maggie got up from her chair and tightly embraced Jim. "Please forgive me."

"There's nothing to forgive, Maggie. I promise to be very careful. Now, why don't we enjoy this evening. I need to get an early start in the morning." Jim wrapped his arm around Maggie's waist, and they went inside the house to explain to Mary why Jim had elected to volunteer for such a dangerous endeavor.

7

She was the runt of the litter. Born in February 1897 in Nepal, high in the Himalayan foothills, Pashir was similar to any other tigress cub. Her mother, Tamil, was a strong, healthy 375-pound tigress that had selected her territory carefully. It was sparsely inhabited by humans, and she had little to fear for her three cubs—two males and one female.

Pashir's father was a hulking 525-pound tiger whose territory overlapped Tamil's. Following a two-week mating period during the preceding November, Tamil separated from her mate and retreated deep into her territory, where she would find peace and tranquillity to give birth to her cubs.

Tamil birthed the three healthy cubs in a dense thicket of scrub oak bushes. There she nurtured her offspring until they were six weeks old. Every evening, Tamil left her cubs to hunt for sambar and chital deer, her favorite prey.

On most nights she returned empty-handed. Sometimes she returned with smaller prey—langur monkeys, jungle fowl, or pheasants. And on rare occasions she was able to return to her cubs with the front portion of a deer for them to share. Often she would have to travel over fifty square miles of territory searching for prey. Despite her incredible stealth, acute hearing and night vision, and ability to use the darkness as cover, she was successful in only one out of every twenty attempts.

When she was able to pull down a large sambar deer, she would eat her fill from the hindquarters of the animal before dragging the remainder of the heavy carcass back to her waiting cubs.

Fortunately, prey was abundant in Tamil's territory, providing plenty of sustenance for her and her cubs.

Pashir, being the smallest of the three cubs, had to fight her larger brothers for the scraps of meat Tamil brought home from her hunts. Often Pashir went without, which caused her to become weaker.

One evening, when Tamil was far away from her den in search of food, a large male leopard stumbled onto the cubs' lair. Having eaten nothing for three days, the hungry predator could not refuse this opportunity. He heard the cubs crying for their mother when he was some distance away, and by focusing on their sound, he was able to locate the den accurately. When he was within fifty feet of the cubs, he crouched in some tall grass to watch and listen attentively for any sign of the tigress. He knew he was no match for an enraged tigress protecting her cubs.

After five minutes, the leopard was convinced the cubs were alone. Slowly and silently, the skillful killer crept toward his unsuspecting prey. When he was ten feet from the cubs, his attention focused on the largest one. The leopard sprang from his hidden position and with lightning speed grasped the large cub by the throat with his deadly fangs while emitting a ferocious roar.

Frightened by the leopard's attack, Pashir and her other brother ran off into the dark to hide. The leopard, with its meal secured in its mouth, ran to a safe location approximately one mile away, where it could devour its meal in peace.

When Tamil returned later that night, she found her cubs missing. The strong scent of the leopard's presence was all she needed to realize what had happened during her absence. She dropped the remains of the chital deer she was carrying and called out to her cubs. There was no response. She called again, listening intently.

After a few seconds, Pashir and her brother overcame their fear and returned their mother's call. Several minutes of searching revealed the place where her remaining cubs were hiding. After Pashir and her brother were shepherded back to the lair, Tamil began to walk in concentric circles out from her den in search of the other male cub, calling out as she did so.

A half-hour later, convinced her other cub was gone, Tamil returned to the den to provide comfort and protection for her remaining two cubs. Pashir was visibly shaken from the ordeal, and calmed down only after several minutes of being caressed and licked by Tamil's raspy tongue. With the loss of her brother, Pashir was now able to eat a larger share of the bounty Tamil brought home, enabling her to achieve a normal growth rate.

The following morning, Tamil grasped Pashir's neck in her mouth just behind her sharp canines and carried her three miles away to a cave located in an area containing numerous large boulders. Then Tamil went back for her other cub. Hoping the cave would provide a safer environment for the cubs, Tamil went out again that evening in her constant pursuit of food.

She had traveled no more than four miles when she heard a chital deer calling out its alarm. Since she was beyond the chital's range of sight, she knew instinctively that another predator was in the area. In short running bursts, she crept her way closer to the chital. When she approached the top of a ridge, she saw the leopard. It was at the bottom of a ravine, feeding on a chital deer it had just killed.

Tamil crept closer as the leopard continued feeding on its prize, unaware of the tiger's presence. When Tamil was within twenty feet of the leopard, she detected the same scent that was present at her den the previous night. Leopards are mortal enemies of tigers, and Tamil knew she must rid her territory of this one.

She readied herself for the inevitable strike. Her tail twitched back and forth, rising upward, then downward. In a flash she sprang from her position, ears laid back, fangs bared, anger replacing any apprehension. She struck the leopard as hard as her 375 pounds of relentless fury could muster, sinking her fangs deep into the back and raking the leopard's sides with her claws. Her ferocious growl accompanied her attack, causing all other animals within hearing distance to flee the terrifying scene. Birds and monkeys squawked and chattered hysterically. In a large ball of hair, fangs, and claws, the two protagonists rolled over and over on the ground in a desperate attempt to deliver the fatal blow.

The large leopard put up a courageous fight, trying with all of its might to dislodge the raging tigress from itself. It kicked with its hind legs, clawed relentlessly, and bit deep gashes in the tiger's exposed flesh. The leopard's penetrating fangs and claws had little effect on Tamil. She knew she was in a life-or-death struggle, and if she lost, her cubs would perish.

With herculean effort, she struggled with the leopard until she eventually saw the opportunity she needed. The leopard moved its head slightly, hoping to get a better grip with its teeth. By doing so, it exposed its throat for one brief second. Tamil lunged with her open jaws, sinking her fangs deep into her target. With all of her might, she applied crushing pressure to the leopard's windpipe, cutting off its oxygen.

The leopard lay writhing on the ground, kicking out with its hind legs in an attempt to free itself from Tamil's fatal grip. Tamil endured the leopard's vicious jabs until the enemy lay still and its breathing ceased. When Tamil finally released her deadly grip, she rolled onto her side to rest. She was breathing heavily, and was bleeding from several puncture wounds left by the leopard's teeth and claws. But she had won, and was proud of her kill!

Rarely do tigers and leopards in the wild kill and eat one another. But to Tamil this was revenge, and what better way to avenge the death of her cub than to devour its assailant?

By the time the early morning mist was burning off the ground, Tamil had devoured the entire rear portion of the leopard. She grabbed it by its throat and began her journey back to her waiting cubs, which were anxiously anticipating the delicacy mom was bringing home.

Pashir enjoyed frolicking with her brother. Their days were filled with endless play. When Tamil was resting with them during the daylight hours, she would swing her tail back and forth, allowing the cubs to attack it. Although the cubs delighted in the game,

Tamil was actually teaching them one of the many aspects of hunting. The training process would last for two years before they were capable of hunting and surviving on their own.

On one occasion, when Pashir and her brother were six months old, they encountered a porcupine wandering near their cave. Although their instincts told them to attack, they were not quite sure how to go about it. The cubs darted in and out, hoping to grasp the prey on its head or neck. Invariably, the porcupine remained slightly quicker than its tormentors, and turned to point its rear toward the cubs before they could do any damage.

During one of her lunges, Pashir got too close to her prey and caught a sharp quill in her nose. She cried out in pain, immediately backing away from the porcupine. Her outcry startled her brother, who gave up his pursuit and gazed quizzically at his sister and the long object protruding from her nostril. Pashir rolled on the ground, trying diligently to remove the painful object. Fortunately, the quill penetrated her skin only one-half inch and she was able to dislodge it. Although she lost her battle with the porcupine that day, she learned a valuable lesson that she never forgot. That was the last time she ever attacked a porcupine.

One month later, Tamil decided it was time to take the cubs along on a hunt. The young ones instinctively knew to follow along behind their mother, and to remain silent. When they approached a ravine one mile from their cave, Tamil stopped dead in her tracks. The cubs could sense trouble, and scurried to a nearby bramble thicket. Directly in front of Tamil, resting next to a stream at the bottom of the ravine, was the cubs' father!

Male tigers, when hungry, will kill and eat tiger cubs, even their own offspring. Tamil sensed her cubs were in mortal danger, and had to do something to dissuade her former mate from endangering them. Garnering all possible courage, she stood her ground and began to hiss menacingly at the large male, signaling an imminent attack. Her only hope was to frighten him away.

He outweighed her by over 125 pounds, and Tamil knew if she engaged in a tooth-and-nail battle with the male, she would end up second best. The hulking male watched Tamil cautiously, trying to determine her intent. He twitched his tail, showing his nervousness. Finally, in an act of desperation, Tamil roared ferociously and charged at her mate with strong determination. The male, deciding he was not really interested in tangling with the enraged female, tore off down the ravine at a fast clip. Tamil, having won her bluff, went back to find her cubs, and they continued on their way looking for prey.

At age two, Pashir and her brother were fully grown, mature tigers able to capture prey on their own without Tamil's assistance. One day, while the two cubs were sleeping near the cave following an exhausting night of hunting, Tamil silently walked away into the forest.

Such is the way of nature in the wild. For two years Tamil had risked her life daily to protect the lives of her cubs. Then one day when she believed they were capable of fending for themselves, she left them on their own. This not only is nature's way of precluding inbreeding, but it allowed Tamil to find another mate to proliferate the species.

Pashir and her brother remained together for two more months, then went their separate ways to stake out their own territories and begin their lives as full-grown tigers. Pashir's brother went east into Nepal while Pashir traveled to the west.

For the next year, Pashir moved around from one location to the next in search of a territory rich in prey and devoid of humans. One evening she was able to kill a large sambar deer, and fed from it until dawn. When the sun peeked above the horizon, she dragged the animal's remains behind a large bush and covered it almost entirely with dry leaves and twigs. She then walked into an open area containing tall, thick grass that would provide her ample safety, and slept for the day.

That evening, when darkness returned, Pashir returned to her kill to eat another meal. As she crouched over the sambar and began to rip huge hunks of flesh off the carcass, she heard a loud sound similar to a thunderclap. Simultaneously, Pashir felt a searing pain in her mouth. The combination of the deafening sound and the piercing pain caused her to leap three feet straight up into the air, then run away as fast as she could. She had never been so frightened.

After she had run nearly a mile and could no longer stand the pain in her mouth, Pashir found a cave to rest in and recover from her wound. Meanwhile, the Nepalese hunter who had shot at the tigress from a tree near the sambar returned home without his trophy.

For the next three days, Pashir remained in the cave and nursed her wound. Every time she attempted to eat anything, she found it difficult to apply much pressure with her jaws. One of her upper canine teeth was broken in half, and the lower canine was completely severed down to the gum. Unable to catch her normal prey, she began to scavenge. First she found the meager remains of a rabbit, which she consumed. Later she found a fish next to the stream she frequented, and ate it.

Slowly she started to regain the use of her injured jaws, but she was losing weight fast. One night, nearly exhausted from hunger, she luckily came across a young leopard feeding on a chital deer it had just killed. Pashir's ferocious growls and menacing gestures convinced the leopard to forfeit its kill to the threatening tigress. When the leopard was out of sight, Pashir gorged herself on the entire chital, then returned to her cave.

The next morning, with a restored energy she had not felt in days, Pashir ventured farther west. For several days she tried to capture her natural prey, but each attempt ended in failure. Although she found some smaller prey and scavenged the remains of prey discarded by other predators, she was constantly hungry and was again becoming thinner.

Then one day, as Pashir rested in some tall grass next to a clearing, an elderly woman walked over toward her and began cutting the grass. Pashir remained motionless as she watched the woman cautiously. Too tired and famished to run away, Pashir continued to observe the woman as she came closer and closer. When the woman grabbed a tuft of grass directly in front of Pashir's nose, the tigress struck at the woman's head with her paw, killing her instantly. Wary of humans by nature, Pashir trotted off to a thicket of bramble bushes seventy yards from where the woman lay dead and rested until dusk.

When daylight diminished, Pashir cautiously returned to the human, crept up to the lifeless body, and sniffed at it. The odor was unpleasant. Then Pashir noticed the dried blood that had trickled from the wounds her claws had made as they slashed open the woman's skull. Pashir gently licked the blood from the gashes. Realizing the kill would help satisfy her raging hunger, Pashir gingerly ate one of the woman's legs. After her hunger was partially satisfied, Pashir went back into the forest to look for other prey.

Two days later, still starving, Pashir returned to the location where she had killed the woman. But the woman was no longer there. She sniffed at the ground and picked up the scent of other humans. She followed their scent to the outskirts of a small village, where she waited patiently for her next meal.

Early next morning, Pashir heard a strange noise coming from the forest. She decided to investigate. Her ears picked up a chopping noise. Being careful to mask her movements, she snaked through tall grass and underbrush. As she closed in on the noise, she stopped momentarily to check the wind current. It was coming from ninety degrees to her right, which made it perpendicular to her and the noise. She altered her approach by moving slightly toward her left, then continued her stalk.

When she was within fifty feet of the noise, she crouched silently in tall grass, scanning to find its origin. Quickly, her eyes locked onto a human chopping branches from a large oak tree. A large elephant was tethered to another tree approximately thirty feet to Pashir's left front. Pashir waited patiently, to ensure that no other humans were present in the area and that the human in the tree and the elephant were unaware of her presence.

Fifteen minutes later, when several leafy branches were scattered on the ground beneath the tree, the human began to descend from the tree. This was the opportunity Pashir was waiting for. She stealthily crept closer to the tree, vigilantly watching the human and the elephant. She kept her body close to the ground so it would be hidden by the tall grass. When she was twenty feet from the tree, she stopped her approach and waited. Her tail twitched in anticipation of the kill, but the rest of her sleek, muscular body was frozen.

When the human was eight feet from the ground, Pashir attacked. In a few bounds she was beneath the tree, stretching upward on her powerful hind legs. With a vicious growl, she clamped her fangs around the human's ankle. The startled human released his grip from the branch he was holding onto and tumbled to the ground. He cried out in agony as Pashir's fangs sank deep into his throat. The cat's massive body pinned him to the ground. She held her grip, waiting for the human's chest to stop heaving.

When the breathing stopped, Pashir released her stranglehold. As her adrenaline subsided, Pashir heard human voices in the distance growing louder and louder. She also noticed that the elephant was extremely agitated and was pulling on the cord attached to its leg. Just then, she saw four humans rounding a bend in the path and heading directly toward her. When the men saw Pashir, they stopped dead in their tracks. Still harboring some fear of humans, Pashir decided to forfeit her kill. Roaring menacingly at the humans, she bounded off in the opposite direction and took refuge in a heavily forested ravine two hundred yards away.

The tigress remained hidden in the ravine for the rest of the day, listening intently to the human voices coming from the direction of her kill. That evening, when the forest was quiet and appeared normal, Pashir returned to her kill. She was ravenous with hunger and cast caution to the wind, hoping her kill was where she had left it earlier in the day. Quickly, she approached the big oak tree, trying her best to mask her movements.

It was now dark, but a quarter moon cast sufficient light to force Pashir to exercise some caution. Again she approached the kill upwind, and the scent of humans filled her nostrils. She crouched low to the ground and crept silently toward the tree. She saw the body lying in the same position as she had left it. She stopped in tall grass, watching and listening carefully for any signs of danger. When convinced that everything was all right, she stood up and walked to her kill.

As soon as Pashir approached the human, she heard the loud thunderclap that had caused her so much discomfort before when she had killed the sambar deer. She jumped into the air and sprinted from the area as fast as her legs could carry her. Meanwhile, the Nepalese villager climbed down from the oak tree with his rusty rifle and inspected the bullet hole he had just put in the dead man's leg.

Pashir learned two valuable lessons from that ordeal—never return to a kill, and immediately following a kill, drag it to a safe area so she could eat her fill without being disturbed.

And so began Pashir's reign of terror as a man-eater. As months went by, she increased the size of her territory in all directions, encompassing many places of human habitation. As the human kills mounted, she became bolder and wiser. Her jaw wound had healed almost perfectly, but her two canine teeth remained deformed. Given her altered diet, however, she did not need them.

Finally, after Pashir had killed over two hundred people in Nepal, the enraged villagers drove her into India. She crossed the Lahaghat River during the winter of 1902-1903, and settled in a rugged section of territory near the village of Champawat, where she resumed killing humans.

Yes, Pashir liked her new territory—plenty of food, several streams containing water year-round, many safe places to hide, and a handsome male tiger whose territory overlapped hers in the west. After she finished eating sixty pounds off her latest human kill, Pashir walked contentedly to the nearby stream to satisfy her thirst from the salty flesh.

**8**

On the evening of 18 July, en route to Champawat, Jim and his entourage stopped at the small village of Pali, approximately twelve miles northwest of Champawat. When they arrived, they found the village in a state of chaos. The villagers were so frightened of the man-eater that they refused to leave their huts when Jim and his men entered the village. Human feces littered the ground outside the huts, and the soil stank of urine. Jim had his men unload the gear and start a fire for cooking dinner. Eventually, Jim noticed some of the villagers peeking out their doors. One man finally summoned enough courage to exit his house and approach Jim.

"Have you come to kill the tiger?" asked the man.

"Yes. Who are you?"

"I am Nhabir, the village headman." He placed the palms of his hands together in front of his face and bowed.

"Pleased to make your acquaintance, Nhabir." Jim returned the gesture of respect. "Is there a stream nearby where we can get some fresh water?"

The headman pointed to the east. "Over there, Sahib—five minutes walk."

Jim continued his conversation with Nhabir until several other villagers overcame their fear and joined them. Jim could see the terror in their eyes and attempted to put them at ease. The village headman offered the use of a vacant hut for Jim and his men.

However, upon seeing the unsanitary condition within the hut, Jim decided to sleep outside for the night.

Realizing he had to do something to gain the villagers' confidence, he asked Nhabir if there was a path nearby that the man-eater used frequently. The headman pointed north to a trail just inside the forest, on which the tiger had been seen on numerous occasions. Armed with that information and his .500 rifle, Jim and two of his men made their way to the path.

The trail was located fifty feet inside the forest, and a portion of it ran parallel to the village. Upon inspection, Jim found several tiger and leopard pug marks in the soft dirt of the trail. He found an ideal spot that the man-eater could easily use to observe the villagers. He then selected a tree to lean against that afforded an excellent view and line of fire in both directions along the path. Jim returned to the village with his men to eat dinner.

During dinner, Jim told the headman of his plan to sit up during the night against the tree, hoping to get a shot at the man-eater. Nhabir thought Jim was a fool and protested vehemently. Despite the headman's objections, at dusk Jim walked back to the tree he had selected and made himself as comfortable as possible.

Two hours later, Jim had to agree with Nhabir—he was crazy to try this foolish endeavor! Although the full moon provided ample visibility, the shadows moving on the ground caused by the wind blowing through the trees left Jim overcome with fear.

Dozens of times he thought he saw the man-eater approaching him, and finally became exhausted from raising his rifle to his shoulder. His pride would not permit him to return to the village, so Jim bit his lip in fear and frustration. The cold air chilled him to the bone. Jim sat beneath the tree, shivering from the cold and fear, until exhaustion from the day's rigorous activities bested him. Around 1 A.M. Jim fell asleep.

The following morning, the headman and three of Jim's men found him fast asleep. When Jim awoke, the headman expressed astonishment that Jim was still alive. As the men walked back to the village for some hot tea and breakfast, Jim swore to himself he would never do anything so stupid again. *In fact*, he thought, *if I ever do that again, I'll only need to take along one bullet—the one I'll shoot myself with for being so bloody stupid!*

Nevertheless, Jim's irrational act had a positive effect on the villagers. Word spread like wildfire that he had survived the night alone in the forest with the man-eater. The villagers thought Jim was blessed with some special karma that made him impervious to the man-eater, and they came out of their huts to touch him on his arms and legs, hoping some would rub off onto them.

By noon the villagers had begun to resume their normal activities. Jim encouraged them to clean and sanitize their huts before any bacterial disease took hold. Most of the villagers had been kept hostage in their small huts by the man-eater's tyranny for over three years. They ventured out only when absolutely necessary—to gather food and water or tend to their livestock. Most of the crops that had been growing in the cultivated land surrounding the village had gone to seed.

Knowing that the villagers had not eaten anything substantial for quite a while and feeling sorry for the children, whose ribs stuck out prominently, Jim asked, "Is there anywhere around here I can shoot a goral (mountain goat)?"

The villagers looked at each other, each one afraid to speak. They were desperately hungry and wanted to take Jim to a remote area where they knew he could shoot a goat, but were still unsure of this stranger. They were also still terrified by the man-eater, and were not about to trust someone just because he had a rifle. How did they know if he was a good hunter? How could they know how brave he was? What if he saw the tiger and ran away, leaving them at the man-eater's mercy? They were well aware of the tiger's ferocity and savage power. This tall, skinny European standing before them did not give them any sense of security.

The villagers stood in silence, not knowing what to say or do. They did not want to offend Jim, but on the other hand, they did not want to place their lives in the hands of an untested stranger. They looked at each other, waiting for someone to tell Jim how they felt. They wanted to tell him that they were scared beyond reason by an animal demon that took the form of a tiger and attacked them relentlessly, no matter which deity they prayed to or how many offerings they made. No one spoke.

Jim, sensing their fear and apprehension, said, "I know you're hungry and haven't eaten because of the man-eater. Please let me help you."

The villagers again looked at each other, but remained quiet. Finally, the headman said, "There are goral along the ridge over there." He pointed to the west, toward the forested hillside adjacent to the ridge on which the village was located.

Jim smiled. "Can someone show me the way?"

The villagers began conversing among themselves, hoping that one of their number would be bold enough to accompany Jim. Out of desperation and hunger, a young man agreed to go. Jim ordered his men to go along, and the group followed the young villager along a path to an open area on the west face of the ridge where they could see the adjacent hillside without obstruction. The young man pointed to a large grassy area near the top of the hill that was surrounded by thick forest.

"Goral!" he announced.

Jim located a tree stump on which he could rest and steady his rifle, then clicked the safety catch off. He scanned the grassy area methodically, looking for a mountain goat. He also asked his men and the villager to help him look. Minutes passed silently as the men continued to peer at the grassy area. No one saw any movement whatsoever.

Finally, Jim saw what he thought was some grass moving slightly and a small patch of white. He pointed to the area and asked if anyone else saw anything. No one did. He did not want to waste a bullet needlessly, so he continued to monitor the site carefully. When he thought he saw the white patch move, he again asked the others for confirmation. No one saw anything.

Trusting his instincts, Jim set his sights for two hundred yards and aimed the old .450 Martini-Henry rifle at the distant white patch. When he felt comfortable with his aim, he slowly squeezed the trigger. The loud crack from the rifle caused the other men to flinch, but they continued to watch the grassy area for the outcome of the shot.

For seconds, nothing happened. Just when Jim thought he had fired at an imaginary target, the grass immediately below where he had aimed began to move. Everyone expressed surprise as they watched the grass continue to part downward toward the bottom of the hill. Seconds later, a goat slid out of the grass down the hill with its legs pointing back up toward the crest. The men were astonished.

As the goat continued to roll to the bottom, it disturbed two other goats resting in the tall grass. Jim threw up his rifle and shot one as it calmed down, then shot the other one as it ran diagonally across the hillside. Soon all three goats were lying at the bottom of the ravine, directly in front of them.

By this time, all the men were jabbering and shouting with joy. They had never seen such an exhibition of marksmanship. The village man was so excited he temporarily forgot about the man-eater. He joined Jim's men and ran to the ravine, where they picked up their prizes and carried them back to the village. Other villagers greeted the entourage as they entered the village, and the throng took the goats to the courtyard, where they were prepared for a feast.

The young villager who had served as Jim's guide was busy telling everyone who would listen about how the sahib had shot the goats at a distance of over a mile with magic bullets and the goats all tumbled down the hill, landing at the sahib's feet. Jim smiled to himself as he listened to the man convincingly tell the others that such a powerful weapon could surely destroy the *shaitan* (devil).

Jim's shooting exhibition had the desired effect, so the next morning some of the villagers agreed to show him where the man-eater's latest attack had taken place. When they arrived at the oak tree, Jim carefully analyzed the man-eater's pug marks, which confirmed that the animal was a tigress, slightly beyond her prime.

He looked up into the tree and saw the branch the woman had clutched onto for dear life. Dark strands of skin from her hands still hung from the branch, swaying in the breeze. Jim shuddered.

He then traced the man-eater's trail to the rock in the ravine where it had waited patiently for the woman to climb down from the tree and seal her fate. Jim followed the trail farther and found a pool of dried blood where the tigress had killed the woman.

Tracing the blood trail up the ravine, Jim located the place where the killer had eaten the woman. Only some of her clothing mixed with splinters of bone remained. Jim helped the villagers collect the remains for a proper cremation ceremony, and they returned to the village.

That afternoon, the villagers took Jim to a nearby field where the man-eater had attacked a woman two weeks earlier. The woman had been working in the field with her sister when the tigress attacked. When the woman heard her sister scream, she turned and saw the animal running off with her sister in its jaws. She immediately ran after the man-eater, brandishing her sickle and yelling at the tigress to release its victim.

The enraged tigress dropped her sister and turned to confront the woman. Fearing for her life, the woman ran back to the village as fast as her legs could carry her. The tragic incident was so harrowing that she had lost her voice. When Jim introduced himself to the woman and told her of his intent to destroy the man-eater, she put her hands together and stooped to touch his feet. Other than the fact that she would not speak a word, she appeared quite normal.

By the end of the day, Jim had gathered considerable information about the man-eater. He had already suspected it to be a large tigress from information he had received from other hunters, and the pug marks he found at the attack sites confirmed it. However, he needed to know what trails it frequently used, what water holes it frequented, any area it might use as its home base, whether it had always been seen alone, etc.

Jim brought along a map of the tigress's territory that indicated all the locations throughout the region where attacks had taken place. When he had finished marking the attack sites on it, he noticed there was no area within the two hundred square miles that had been spared by the tigress. Not only was the area rugged and treacherous, it was also clustered throughout with small enclaves of families who were trying to eke out an existence in this heavily forested country. Jim sighed in frustration as he thought about the monumental task that lay before him.

The information he was able to glean from the villagers was of negligible value. Those who had seen the tigress claimed she was alone, and no one knew whether she had a home base or frequented one area more than any other.

Judging from what Jim was told, the man-eater traveled extensively throughout her domain, attacking at will. The numerous crosses Jim had placed on his map certainly confirmed that! Jim also knew the tigress never returned to a kill, human or animal. This would not only make her more difficult to catch, but had also caused the human death toll to mount faster. By not returning to her kills for additional meals, the tigress had to kill more frequently. Also, her leaving half-eaten remains of humans scattered around the countryside for others to see had terrified these poor villagers beyond comprehension. Jim could only empathize with their plight and wait for the next tragedy to occur.

The next day, while Jim was having breakfast with his men, a *cooee* report was relayed to the village. Messages were normally relayed from village to village by messengers on foot. However, when people were in a hurry or threatened by a man-eater, messages were sometimes shouted (*cooee*) from the edge of a village by someone who climbed into a tree or stood on a tall rock. The villager who had received this report slid down the steep embankment on the outskirts of the village and came running toward Jim.

"Sahib! The tiger attacked again . . . a small village . . . that direction!" He was pointing due east and trying to catch his breath.

"How long ago?"

"Just this morning! Hurry, Sahib!"

Jim barked orders to his men, who were already in motion. He quickly grabbed his rifles and cartridges, and began walking at a brisk pace with three of his men trailing him. One of the men carried Jim's backup rifle and extra ammunition. The two others carried provisions that would last them for two days.

Jim was fairly familiar with this territory. He had visited the area on previous hunting expeditions. Therefore, with the aid of his detailed map, he knew every trail and population enclave in the region. He suspected the attack had occurred at a small village on a ridge overlooking a small river. He cautioned his men to be observant, and the four men covered the distance in two hours.

When they approached the village, Jim heard the mournful wailing of the native women. He immediately noticed three distressed women grieving over their loss and the village menfolk trying to console them. Jim stood twenty feet away from the group until one of the men noticed him. When Jim announced who he was and why he was there, the men went over to greet him.

"Sahib, you've arrived in time to see us destroy the demon," one of the men exclaimed.

"You've captured the tiger?"

"Yes, Sahib. Come look!"

The group led Jim and his men to the far end of the village, where he saw a frightened Indian tethered to a wooden post, cursing at his tormentors. Other villagers were stacking sticks and straw beneath the bound man's feet, preparing to incinerate the helpless being. Jim knew instantly what was happening. He quickly fired his rifle into the air to stop the procedure, and the throng turned toward Jim, puzzled to see him standing there.

"Release that man—NOW!" Jim stood erect with fire in his eyes.

Surprised by Jim's outburst, the man who had escorted him to the site replied, "But Sahib, he is the evil spirit who preys upon our families in the form of a tiger. He must be destroyed by fire to release the spell."

Jim had heard of this kind of thing happening before in villages plagued by a man-eater, but this was the first time he'd been a witness to it.

"This man is not an evil spirit," bellowed Jim. "He is flesh and blood like you and me. Your enemy is a tiger—just a tiger that for some reason eats human flesh instead of animals. When I kill the tiger, I will show you that it is only an animal like all other tigers—not an evil spirit. Now untie that poor man and let him go."

The man next to Jim signaled the quieted group, who quickly untied the man's bonds. As soon as he was free, the stranger, who had picked the wrong time to be traveling through the area, ran off down the trail, showing a clean pair of heels. Jim cringed to think what might have happened if he had not arrived at the village when he did.

"We are sorry, Sahib," the man next to Jim said sheepishly.

Although Jim respected and tried hard to understand the superstitions and rituals in which most of the hillfolk believed, he could not condone the taking of an innocent life to appease those beliefs.

When the situation had calmed, Jim asked about the tiger attack. Reportedly, the tigress had attacked a young girl who was gathering sticks just outside the village at around 7 A.M. The animal bounded away with the girl, holding her by her side. The girl was still alive when she was carried away, screaming for help.

The image Jim conjured up in his mind was horrifying. He only hoped that the girl had died quickly and mercifully when the tigress got out of sight. He asked that the men show him the location of the attack, but they were too frightened to do so. Rather, they pointed in the right direction and indicated it had occurred next to a large ficus tree. Jim and his men quickly walked in that direction, and when they were at the edge of the village, Jim spotted the tree.

As he approached it, he could not help but notice the bundle of sticks scattered on the ground, mixed with footprints and pug marks. A quick observation and analysis revealed the direction in which the tigress had departed the area. The trail was now over three hours old, so Jim lost no time in following up the cat's trail.

Since the tigress had the girl by the side, there were no drag marks in the dirt. Nevertheless, the man-eater's prints were clear enough for Jim to track her.

Jim followed the prints along the path for nearly 150 yards. When he rounded a bend in the trail, he noticed large splashes of blood on the ground. Looking carefully at the telltale signs in the dirt, he realized the tigress had released her grip on her victim's side and grasped the girl by the throat or neck. Blood had oozed from the puncture wounds when the tigress removed her fangs. Also, now there were marks where the girl's feet had dragged alongside the tiger. As grisly as the scene was, Jim found some consolation in knowing that the girl would most certainly be dead by now.

For the next three hours, Jim pursued the tigress relentlessly over all types of terrain. He followed the tracks along trails, through open fields, across streambeds, and into dense forest containing thick foliage and creeper vines. When visibility was limited, he was forced to slow his pursuit, sometimes to a snail's pace.

He remembered what Peter had told him prior to his departure from Naini Tal, so he treated every bush, boulder, and patch of tall grass as a possible ambush site. At 4:10 P.M., the tracks led Jim right up to a large clearing containing shoulder-high grass. Jim suspected the tigress was hiding in the grass, eating her victim. Knowing it would be suicidal to enter the area, Jim skirted the entire field, looking for any sign of the tigress's departure from it. He found nothing.

Convinced the tigress was still in the tall grass, Jim contemplated his options: 1) He could not muster enough men to conduct a "beat." Besides, it was too late in the day to arrange it. 2) He could not enter the tall grass on foot because visibility was almost negligible and he would most likely get himself killed. 3) He could return to the village for the night and return in the morning. However, the tigress would surely be long gone by then. 4) He and his men could build a hasty *machan* (blind) in one of the trees adjacent to the grassy area, where he could stay the night in hopes of getting a shot at the tigress if she exited the area.

After a short study of the area and discussing the situation with his men, Jim decided to find a tree for a *machan*. Since the grassy area encompassed several acres, Jim was hard-pressed to find a tree that would afford him good visibility over the entire area. One side of the grassy area adjoined forest, so Jim selected a tree on that side, believing the tigress would most likely enter the forest when she exited the grass.

With Jim keeping a sharp lookout, his men built a *machan* from foliage and some rope they had brought along. When it was finished, Jim instructed them to return to the village for the night, and to take his spare rifle with them for protection. Jim climbed into the *machan* and watched his men walk out of sight. He then pulled out his biscuits and began eating them while listening to what the forest creatures had to say about the situation.

When he had finished the biscuits, he pelted the grassy area to his front with several stones his men had gathered for him before they left. Sufficient daylight remained for him to detect the tigress moving through the grass if she was disturbed by the stones, which would enable Jim to get off a shot. Though he threw twenty-two stones throughout the area, Jim did not detect any movement whatsoever. He then sat back in his *machan* to get more comfortable, and waited for the night's cloak of darkness to arrive. Soon the tranquil but haunting sounds of the night engulfed Jim's senses.

When dawn was breaking the following morning, Jim was dismayed that he had neither seen nor heard any sign of the tigress throughout the night. He scanned the area to his front one more time, then began to climb down from the *machan* to stretch his cramped legs.

As soon as his feet touched the ground, he sensed danger—not in the field but rather in the forest! Placing his rifle to his shoulder, he carefully scoured every square inch he could see with his eyes. Suddenly, he noticed some tall grass next to a large bush about twenty feet from the tree returning to an upright position.

He slowly walked toward the bush, but at a forty-five-degree angle to it, keeping his rifle to his shoulder. When he could see behind the bush and was convinced it was safe to approach, he went to investigate. As he knelt where the grass had sprung up, he was shocked to see the tigress's pug marks clearly imprinted in the soft earth. The man-eater had been lying behind the bush watching his every move while he was in the *machan*!

Jim sensed he was still in danger. Still kneeling, he rapidly swung his rifle around to the right with the barrels pointing upward at a sixty-degree angle. He fixed his eyes on a clump of dense shrubs located at the top of a small hill next to him. The bushes agitated violently, then several dislodged pebbles rolled down the hill toward him. Jim aimed at the bush and squeezed the trigger, sending a heavy bullet directly through the center of the bush. He waited silently, listening intently to a large animal crashing away through the forest.

After a few minutes, Jim slowly crept up the hill, keeping his rifle trained on the bushes. When he reached the top, he could see no sign of the tigress. After scanning the immediate area, he walked over to the bushes and found more pug marks. He carefully followed her tracks away from the bushes, looking for bloodstains on the ground. There were none.

Realizing that his men probably had heard his gunshot and would be heading toward his location, Jim decided to quickly make his way back to the village in case the tigress tried to intercept his men.

**9**

Knowing that humans were trailing her, Pashir decided to seek refuge in a large area of tall grass where she would be difficult to detect. She found a small depression near the center of the grassy area and released her grip on her prey, watching the kill fall lifeless to the ground. Noticing the blood flowing from the exposed skin, Pashir licked at the crimson liquid until it was gone. She lay next to her kill and waited patiently to determine whether the pursuing humans would enter the grassy area. She could hear their voices, but they remained outside the area.

A little later, she heard three humans doing something next to the forest's edge. Later she saw one of the humans climb into a large tree. He had one of those long sticks—the kind that sounded like thunder and caused her so much pain. Pashir crouched lower, but kept her attention focused on the man in the tree. When all was quiet again, she saw the man put down the stick and begin eating something. Pashir decided to eat her fill from her kill while she had the chance. She grasped the girl's left upper thigh and bit through it effortlessly. Blood poured from the leg and torso. Pashir commenced tearing huge hunks of flesh from the meatier portion of the leg, crunching the bone into small pieces before swallowing. She ate down to the ankle, then bit off the other leg just below the buttocks. Occasionally, Pashir licked the spilled blood and even ate the blood-soaked clothing.

As she was finishing the second leg, she heard a thumping noise on the ground to her left. She remained motionless as she heard another thump, then another. She raised her head slightly and saw the man in the tree throwing objects into the field. Convinced she was in no danger, she resumed eating the fleshy buttocks. When a stone landed five feet from her, she glanced over at it, then went back to her business.

When she had finished her meal, the only portions remaining were one of the girl's feet, the toes from her other foot, several fingers, and the upper part of her skull with her long, black hair still attached. Thirsty from eating the salty flesh, Pashir silently exited the field on the opposite side from where the human sat in the tree. It was dark, and the moon had not yet come up, allowing Pashir to sneak away without being detected. She circled the field out of sight of the man, and headed for a small stream in the forest. After quenching her thirst, Pashir felt compelled to stalk the human. She silently crept through the forest until she was about one hundred feet directly behind the man.

Using bushes and trees for concealment, Pashir crept up to a large bush approximately twenty feet behind the tree—an excellent place from which to launch her attack when the human descended. Although her hunger had been satisfied, this was an opportunity too good to pass. She quietly lay down behind the bush, keeping her attention focused on the human. He was too high in the tree for her to climb or leap up. A cool wind was coming off the field into the forest, which would mask her scent from the human. Everything was perfect. So Pashir waited patiently.

When daylight came, Pashir became anxious. Since the human would be able to see her approach the tree, she had to exercise caution. She saw the human start to descend the tree. Pashir tensed her muscles, and her tail began to twitch back and forth. The human was fifteen feet from the ground. A little lower, and Pashir would be able to reach him by fully extending herself. Just when Pashir was ready to launch her fateful attack, the human swung around to the opposite side of the tree and was now facing her!

Disgruntled, Pashir decided to leave her position and circle back to the bushes on top of the hill where she would have a better vantage point. As she reached the place, she saw the man walking slowly, facing the bush she had just left. Pashir crouched and patiently waited for another opportunity to attack. When the human was kneeling at the bush looking at the ground, Pashir began twitching her tail again. Ready to spring, she caught herself as the human suddenly looked up at her. She scrambled from the bushes just as the thunderclap roared. Frightened by her narrow escape, Pashir retreated deep into the forest to rest for the remainder of the day. Tomorrow she would move to another location and hunt again.

O n his way back to the small village, Jim shivered at the thought of the tigress watching him all night from the bushes. He realized what could have happened if he had not descended from the tree on the side opposite the man-eater. If he had come down with his back *toward* the tigress, he would most likely have become the man-eater's latest statistic! He thought some more about his conversation with Peter: " . . . like a phantom . . . appears and disappears mysteriously." Jim made a mental note to exercise more caution in the future.

When he returned to the village, he found his men preparing breakfast.

"Did you hear my shot a while ago?"

"Yes, Sahib," answered one, "but you told us not to come unless we heard three shots."

"Good! You did the right thing. I shot at the tigress, but missed her. She ran off, and could be anywhere. If you had come into the forest looking for me, you might have been killed."

Jim ate breakfast with his men, then stood guard while the villagers sanitized their huts and tended to their crops and livestock. When they had gathered ample firewood and fodder for their cattle, Jim bade them farewell. They beseeched him to stay, but he wanted to return to Pali.

Knowing that the tigress relocated from one area to another following each kill, Jim tried to assure the villagers that it was unlikely she would strike again in their village anytime soon. His words provided little assurance to these poor people. They were terrorized out of their wits and wanted full-time protection.

Jim finally convinced them that he had to protect the entire territory, and needed to be at Champawat to reduce travel time when the tigress struck again. He knew that Champawat was near the center of the man-eater's territory and would be the best location for his base camp.

As he and his men departed the village, Jim saw the forlorn expression on the villagers' faces. As badly as he felt, however, he knew he had to stick to his plan if he was going to have any chance of destroying the man-eater. He then returned to Pali, to gather up his other men and equipment for their journey to Champawat. There, Jim told the rest of his men and the villagers what had happened during his absence. When he had finished his story, the headman smiled graciously, then turned and walked away. He had heard this same story many times before from other hunters over the previous four years, and hearing it again from Jim only added to his disappointment.

He and most of the other villagers believed the tigress was a myth, a vision of death that had brought devastation and despair to their lives because of something someone did or said to offend the spirits. Tigers, they believed, were spirits of the forest, protecting it and its inhabitants. Once offended, though, the tiger would seek vengeance until atonement had been made. Such was the case with the Champawat man-eater. No human could kill it, they believed, until it had punished all transgressors.

Jim had the same difficulty convincing the Pali villagers of his intention to leave, but he knew the tigress was heading east *toward* Champawat, and that was the direction he needed to go. As Jim was walking out of the village, he saw the pleading look in the villagers' eyes. It gave him a heavy heart.

On the path to Champawat, Jim was joined by other travelers heading in the same direction. When Jim told them the purpose of his visit, one man revealed a tragic tale that had occurred two months earlier:

"We were traveling along this same path to the bazaar at Champawat when we heard a woman's anguished cries for help. We immediately stopped to determine the direction of the cries, and realized they were coming from the valley below us. When we looked down, we saw a tiger carrying a woman by the small of her back. Her hair was dragging along the ground, and she was beating her chest, pleading for help.

"We were so frightened, we could do nothing. What can men do when they are so frightened? We ran to the village, collected more men with weapons, and followed the tiger's tracks until we found the woman. We arrived too late. She was lying dead on a rock, completely naked. We covered her body with our loin cloths and carried her back to the village."

The man sighed. "She was only sixteen."

Jim felt depressed after hearing the story. He marveled at how anyone who had experienced such a gruesome sight could ever leave the security of his house until the man-eater had been destroyed. But life must go on, despite setbacks and tragedies.

When Jim arrived at Champawat, he found it to be in the same state as Pali was. While his men were setting up camp, he talked with the villagers about the man-eater. One man suggested Jim stay at a small bungalow a few miles away, in an area the man-eater frequented. These bungalows, scattered throughout the region, had been built by the government for use by government personnel who were traveling on official business.

The following morning, Jim walked to the bungalow and talked to the people there about the man-eater. They were not much help, and after going on a couple of wild-goose chases, Jim returned that evening to sleep at the bungalow. An Indian official who was supposed to spend the night with Jim in the bungalow decided against staying—despite Jim's protests of his traveling at night through a man-eater's territory. Jim found out that night why the man was so adamant about taking his chances with the man-eater rather than staying the night in the bungalow.

At 3 A.M., Jim awoke from a sound sleep. The small flame in his hurricane lamp on the nightstand had been extinguished, and it was pitch-black in the room. Suddenly, he felt an eerie sensation that something evil was in the room. He then heard a strange "clunking" noise that sent shivers up and down his spine. The noise was similar to someone dropping a heavy object on the floor.

Jim peered into the darkness to try to determine the source of the noise. "Who's there?" he asked sternly. The noise did not repeat itself—the room was starkly silent. When Jim started to believe his imagination was running wild on him, he saw it: A glowing blue vapor came into view at the end of his bed. It was about the shape and size of a man and had small, dark circles where the eyes, nose, and mouth would normally have been.

Jim gasped in horror. He had heard tales about some of these bungalows being haunted, but he discounted them as merely someone's active imagination. He rubbed his eyes and with a shaky voice asked, "Who are you?"

There was no answer. The vision remained at the foot of the bed, stationary. It appeared translucent, its intensity waxing and waning. Jim's immediate reaction was to shoot and ask questions later, but his rifle was propped against the wall near the door.

When Jim felt a cold, clammy sensation creeping up his legs from his feet, he decided he was overstaying his welcome. In one quick movement, he sprang from the bed and bolted to the door, grabbed his rifle, and spun around to face the apparition.

It was gone. The room was in total darkness again. The only sound Jim could hear was his sharp, heavy breathing. His heart was pounding like never before as he continued to train his rifle toward the bed. As Jim began to calm down, he realized he had a difficult decision to make. He could go outside for the rest of the night and worry about the man-eater attacking him, or stay indoors and face whatever it was he'd seen and felt only minutes earlier.

Jim decided to remain inside the bungalow, but with the light burning brightly. Slowly he walked to the nightstand, placed his rifle on the bed, and with trembling hands lit the hurricane lamp.

When light permeated the room, he sighed and sat on a chair next to the nightstand with his rifle on his lap. He sat in the chair smoking cigarettes until dawn, wide awake.

During the following two days, Jim prepared himself for the next inevitable tiger attack by cleaning his weapons and checking his gear and ammunition. Longing for a change of diet, he asked the villagers if there was a place nearby where he could catch some fish. The village headman told Jim about a deep pond formed by a natural dam approximately three miles downstream from the village. An avid fisherman, Jim grabbed his bamboo fly rod and his box of hand-tied flies and set off for the pond. As a security precaution, he had one of his men bring along Jim's rifle and ammunition. Jim also decided to take along his horse, to help carry back the plunder if he got lucky.

It was a beautiful morning. The sky was a brilliant cornflower blue, and the sunshine reflecting off the snowcapped peaks of the Himalayas in the distance was a glorious sight to behold. Jim listened to the birds chirping and singing as he walked along the trail, attempting to identify each bird by its sound. He was successful in all attempts, with two exceptions. In both cases, the birds' sweet melody was new to Jim, and his efforts to see the tiny creatures were unsuccessful. Enraptured by the stunning sights and sounds along the way, he nearly forgot about the man-eater.

As he rounded a bend in the trail that ran adjacent to the stream, he saw the pond straightaway. The stream went down a deep embankment similar to a waterfall, pouring into the near end of the pond. At the far end, the excess water spilled over the dam and continued its winding journey to the Ladhya River some ten miles away. The pond was located in a deep ravine, with steep banks on both sides climbing ridges thirty to fifty feet high. The area was heavily forested, producing a tranquil setting. The dimensions of the pond itself were approximately eighty yards long and thirty yards wide at the center.

Jim found a fairly flat place to stand near the center and gazed at the beauty of the setting. The water was a deep blue, as clear and smooth as a sheet of glass. The only ripples were at the end where the water cascaded down the large boulders from upstream. The reflections in the water of the trees and boulders on the opposite side had a mesmerizing effect.

Jim assembled his three-piece rod, attached the reel, threaded the line through the eyelets, and selected a fly from the small box. He was standing in a clearing with just enough open space to allow him to effectively cast the tiny fly out onto the water. On the third cast, a large fish took the fly and fought valiantly. Five minutes later, Jim landed a twelve-pound *mahseer*, one of his favorite fish. Not only was it tasty, but was also known for its fight at the end of a line.

By 11 A.M., Jim had caught eleven large *mahseer*, enough to feed most of the village. He promised himself he would call it a day after catching one more. He deftly flipped the fly out into the water again and watched it float lazily toward the dam. Suddenly, the surface broke apart and the fly disappeared. Jim struck and knew instantly he had his hands full.

Line screamed from his reel as the large fish darted for the dam. Jim's line was only twenty-pound test, and he quickly realized that the fish on the other end weighed far more than his line strength. He waited helplessly as the fish continued stripping the line from his reel, and just when only a few feet of line remained, the fish stopped pulling.

Slowly and cautiously, Jim began to retrieve line. Every time he reeled some in, his worthy opponent made another run toward the dam, taking line with it.

After playing the fish for over forty minutes, Jim was nearing exhaustion. Fortunately, so was the fish. Again Jim retrieved some line, ready to release it if the fish took off. However, this time the fish came along—reluctantly, tugging periodically just to let Jim know it was not yet ready to surrender.

Jim's arched rod strained from the tension placed on it, and the tip jerked spastically. Paanu, Jim's assistant, jumped up and down on the bank in excitement, encouraging Jim to bring in the "monster." The fish stayed deep, but continued to come closer.

Jim fervently hoped he would at least be able to see the fish, even if he lost it.

He finally maneuvered the fish to within fifteen feet of the shore. There was a deep drop-off at that location, and the fish stayed near the bottom. Jim kept tension on the line, wondering what to do next. He looked at Paanu for guidance, but Paanu only grinned his broad, toothless smile, gesturing for Jim to pull harder.

Wanting to return to the village, Jim became impatient. Applying more pressure, he began to wrestle the fish up off the bottom. Suddenly, the line went slack. Two seconds later, the big fish broke water ten feet away with a loud splash. Jim saw the huge back as its dorsal fin knifed through the water. Then, with a tremendous splash from its plate-sized tail, the fish lunged for the dam again, snapping the line.

Jim and Paanu stared at the water in silence for nearly a minute. Then they looked at each other and broke out laughing. Jim estimated the *mahseer* that got away weighed close to fifty pounds, and made a promise to himself to challenge the champion again if he ever got the opportunity.

As soon as Jim and Paanu returned to Champawat with their catch, the village headman informed Jim of the man-eater's latest attack, just northwest of the town.

**11**

When Jim and his men arrived at the small village four miles northwest of Champawat, they found the inhabitants in a state of uproar and fear. Jim was immediately ushered to a small mud-and-thatch hut, where lay the man-eater's most recent victim. When Jim entered the hut, the stench of blood mixed with human waste overwhelmed him.

The victim, a young man, was still alive—barely. He had massive claw marks on his left shoulder that extended several inches down his back. Congealed blood clotted the right side of his head, where the tigress had grabbed him with her fangs. His breathing was rough and intermittent. Jim requested some boiling water to clean the wounds, and asked the headman to have someone sanitize the room.

When the hot water was brought, Jim washed the wounds. As he cleaned the victim's head, he noticed the right eye was punctured and one ear was missing. He applied antiseptic lotion he had brought with him to the wounds, and wrapped them with bandages. He did the best he could with what he had, but felt it was unlikely that the man would survive.

It would be futile to go after the tigress right then, so Jim made some tea and got acquainted with the local populace. The village consisted of thirty-seven people in several different families. Over the previous four years, the tigress had claimed thirteen of their number. It was certainly understandable why the remaining members were so terrorized. Jim knew the futility of advising these people to relocate to an area outside the man-eater's territory. Like all the other hill tribes throughout this area, they had lived here all their lives and could not conceive of living elsewhere, even temporarily.

Jim finished his tea, and asked the headman if he would show Jim the location of the attack. At first reluctant, the headman acquiesced. When they arrived at the attack scene, it did not take Jim long to figure out what had happened.

The man had been gathering firewood in a forested area 150 feet from the village when the tigress crept up behind and attacked him. She had approached her victim at great speed and lunged at the man, causing both of them to tumble down a steep embankment. During the fall, the tigress had lost her hold on the victim's head, become disoriented, and run off. Upon seeing the tigress's pug marks, Jim knew in an instant she was the man-eater.

Thirty feet from the attack location, Jim found the place where the tigress had lain in wait behind some bushes and launched her attack. The victim's blood was smeared on the ground at the top and bottom of the hill. Since the tigress had been denied her meal, Jim decided to build a *machan* in a nearby oak tree, hoping she would return during the night.

An hour later when the *machan* was finished, Jim and the men returned to the village for dinner. While Jim was eating, a middle-aged man approached whose face was grotesquely disfigured. Just looking at the man caused Jim to lose his appetite. Hair was missing from half of his head, and the right side of his face was covered with sagging, wrinkled scar tissue. Jim listened in horror as the man told his story:

"Sahib, four years ago I was with my son collecting fodder for our cattle. We were on a hill next to a ravine nearly a mile from here. When I bent over to cut some tall grass, a tiger attacked me from the large rocks where it was hiding. The attack forced me to fall near the edge of the ravine. Part of my head was in the tiger's mouth, and it was lying on top of me with its paws on my chest. I was in great pain, and the tiger was growling.

"I grabbed a tree next to me and raised my knees up toward my head. I did this very slowly so I would not make the tiger more angry. I then placed my feet under the tiger's stomach on each side. With all my strength, I lifted the tiger with my legs, causing it to go over the ridge and down into the ravine. I held onto the tree as tightly as I could so I would not fall with the tiger. This I was able to do, but the tiger took half of my face with it. My son was standing only ten feet from me when this happened, and was too frightened to move. The tiger ran away after it fell into the ravine, and my son helped me home.

"For two months I lay in bed thinking I was going to die. I lost much blood and was suffering from many wounds. One night, I felt so much pain that I called all my friends and family to my bedside to bid them farewell. I thought it was my last night to live. The next morning when I awoke, a miracle happened. I felt much better, and within three days, I was up and walking again."

Jim was astonished. To lift a four-hundred-pound tiger off you would take tremendous strength and courage. Nevertheless, the man's immense size and scars gave ample credibility to his story.

"You are very brave."

"No, Sahib. Anyone would have done the same to save himself. I wanted to live, and I knew the only way I would survive was to make the tiger fall down the hill."

Jim knew the man was only being modest, a trait common among these simple people. Very few victims would have had the strength or forethought to implement such an endeavor while pinned down by a large tiger. Jim stood and began to walk to the *machan*, where he would spend the night. After hearing the man's story and seeing his face, Jim kept the rifle's safety off until he was sitting in the *machan*.

The night passed without incident, but throughout it Jim had an eerie feeling he was being watched. As the sun began to rise, he descended from the tree in a spiral fashion, keeping a sharp lookout for any sign of the tigress. Once on the ground, he walked in concentric circles away from the oak tree to determine if there was any rationale for his uneasiness during the night.

Although he believed he was not in any immediate danger, he kept the safety off and stayed alert. He approached a large fallen tree forty feet from the oak and noticed an area of grass that was matted down on the far side. Upon closer observation, he saw the tigress's pug marks leading to and away from the large log! There was no telling how long ago she had departed the area, so Jim returned to the village slowly and carefully.

He spent the next two days at the village, hoping to entice the tigress out into the open. Each evening, he sat up over goats, buffalo, or cattle he placed beneath the *machan*. Even though he knew that other hunters before him had never had any luck with such bait, Jim still felt compelled to try. It did not work for him either. During the two days, he neither saw nor heard about the tigress.

On the morning of the third day, Jim and his men were packing for their return to Champawat when a *cooee* call indicated there had been a tiger attack at a small village to the east. Jim quickly finished his preparations, and he and his men set off briskly down the trail.

An hour and a half later, they were met at the edge of the village by the headman. He was in such a panic that Jim had to calm him down before he could understand what had happened.

The headman pointed. "Sahib, the tiger attacked a group of villagers tending their livestock just outside of the village and carried a young man off."

Grabbing his rifle, Jim instructed two of his men to go with him to the attack site. When they arrived, Jim took only seconds to determine in which direction the tigress had gone with her victim. Not wanting to waste any time, Jim began his pursuit.

The man-eater's tracks led him two miles away from the village to a stream several feet wide at the bottom of a forested ravine. The tigress had not repositioned her grip on her victim, so there were only her pug marks and an occasional drag line to follow. The stream was fairly shallow, with fast-running water maneuvering its way around rocks and boulders. Jim walked across the stream to the other side, hoping to pick up the tracks. There were none, indicating the tigress had gone up or downstream for a distance before exiting the water. Jim instructed his two men to look upstream while he went downstream.

Ten minutes later, his men shouted that they had found where the tigress had exited the stream into thick bramble bushes containing long, sharp nettles. On one thorn, Jim noticed a clump of blood-caked black hair from the victim.

The trail continued through dense forest and undergrowth until they arrived at a large open area containing huge boulders. The area was approximately 200 feet long by 150 feet wide, strewn throughout with hundreds of boulders ranging in height from four feet to fifteen feet. Numerous narrow trails were interlaced among the boulders in a large maze.

As Jim and his men entered the area, the tigress growled menacingly at them. Listening to her threats amplified in the boulders sent shivers of fear up Jim's spine. He looked at his men, hoping they would know from which direction the sound came. When they pointed in different directions, he decided for safety's sake to shepherd them back out of the area.

Jim stood with his men near the edge of the forest, contemplating his predicament. Attempting to locate the tigress in the rocky maze with his men would only jeopardize their lives. If he returned to the village, he would lose the chance of getting a shot at the tigress. He decided to climb a tree, hoping to see the cat. Selecting the tallest tree he could find that overlooked the open area, he began his ascent.

On his way up, he recalled an incident that had happened at age fourteen, while he was assigned to his youth military training company. Crusty ol' Sarge, who delighted in the use of intimidation and humiliation, overheard Jim refer to his rifle as his "gun." Sarge decided to teach young Jim a lesson he would remember for the rest of his life. Standing in front of his comrades, Jim had to hold his rifle up with his right hand and, with his left hand holding onto his crotch, recite twenty times, "This is my rifle, this is my gun; this is for killing, this is for fun."

Despite the fact that no one in his company had been exempted from ol' Sarge's sadistic antics, Jim was nevertheless extremely embarrassed over the incident. Although he despised Sarge at the time, in retrospect he had to admit that the old soldier had taught him some valuable lessons. Jim excelled in marksmanship, and the camouflage and survival techniques he had learned were indispensable for hunting India's newest "enemy"—man-eating tigers and leopards.

So, higher and higher Jim ascended, all the while repeating the phrase that had endeared him so much to ol' Sarge. When he reached the highest branch he could get to without endangering his life, he lowered the rope he had with him to his men. They tied the rope to the rifle stock, and Jim carefully pulled the weapon up to him. He instructed his men to climb the tree to a height of twenty feet, then he scanned the open area methodically. However, there were so many boulders scattered throughout the area that Jim could see the ground only in a few places. He noticed a large, flat boulder near the center of the area that was higher than the surrounding ones—a perfect vantage point from which to see in all directions. With the boulder as his next destination, Jim lowered his rifle and climbed back down.

He left his men comfortably settled in the tree as he proceeded to the flat boulder. When he was nearly thirty feet inside the rocky area, the tigress bellowed her low, bone-chilling warning again. Despite Jim's fear, he was encouraged that she was still in the area.

Inch by inch Jim crept alongside the boulders to his destination, frequently stopping to listen and watch for the tigress and to catch his breath. Creeping silently through a cluster of tall boulders, knowing a man-eating tiger is somewhere in the vicinity, is terribly unnerving. No air currents blew among the rocks, so Jim had to prepare himself for an attack from all directions.

Forty-five minutes later, he reached the boulder, quickly slung his rifle over his shoulder, and climbed to the top. He peered over the area, discouraged that the rock did not afford the clear field of vision for which he had hoped. Most of the trails were still hidden by the obstructions. Still shaken from his trek, he sat down and lit a cigarette to calm his nerves. He looked over at his men to see whether they had seen the tigress. No such luck. He inhaled a deep breath and surveyed the area again. He had not heard from the tigress since her last warning nearly an hour earlier. This did not mean, however, that she had departed the area.

Suddenly, Jim's eye caught something on the ground straight up one of the paths leading away from his boulder. He squinted his eyes in the sunlight, trying to make it out. Shielding the sun from his eyes, Jim realized the object was a human foot!

He waited patiently to see if the foot moved, which would indicate the tigress was feeding on the body. Twice Jim thought the foot agitated slightly, but he was not sure. He knew that if he stared at an object long enough, it would sometimes appear to move even though it had not.

Not wanting to waste more time, Jim slid from the rock and slowly crept toward the exposed foot. When he was within fifteen feet, he stopped to determine the best way to approach without being seen by the tigress if she was lying next to her kill. He decided to inch his way around an adjacent boulder, which would place him about ten feet from the body and give him a clear shot at the tigress.

Jim eased his way through the cramped space between two large boulders until he could see the victim's foot again. Slowly he stuck his head out beyond the rock until he could see more of the victim's lifeless body. He could not see the tigress, which caused him to shudder with fear. *If she is not at her kill,* he thought, *where is she?*

After waiting in silence for a minute, Jim cautiously approached the corpse. He wanted to look away from the carnage left behind by the man-eater, but his eyes were forcibly drawn to it. Stripped of every bit of dignity, the nude, twisted, bloody remains mixed with the stench of death would have caused the most battle-hardened soldier to gag. His eyes watering, Jim forced back the nausea.

He quickly scrambled up to the top of a rock to regain his composure. As he gulped large breaths of air into his lungs, he thought about his options. There were no suitable places in the vicinity to sit up over the corpse, and it was too dangerous to drag the remains to another location. The man-eater could still be in the area, or she could have abandoned her kill and be miles away.

Jim looked dejectedly at the setting sun and realized he had only one course of action—to get himself and his men back to safety. Regretfully, he had to leave the remains behind. If the tigress was still lurking among the boulders, he would need every advantage he had to make it back through the maze in one piece. Cursing his luck, Jim slowly made his way back to his waiting men.

## 12

The next day Jim was back at Champawat, thoroughly frustrated. He had tried everything he knew to engage the man-eater, but nothing worked. In fact, Jim never even saw the tigress. She continued to strike at random, drag her victim to a safe location, eat her fill, then move on to another location. On those occasions when Jim was hot on her heels in pursuit, she simply abandoned her kill and escaped. This situation resulted in more frequent attacks, which caused Jim considerable consternation. He kept an accurate log of each attack, noting the time of day, date, exact location, and the age and sex of every victim, hoping to uncover something that would give him an edge. He could find nothing.

Jim had every right to feel frustrated and angry. He could not help thinking that his futile efforts were only making matters worse and driving up the horrifying death count. As he waited at Champawat for the next report on the killer, he contemplated his situation.

He realized he had only three advantages over the tigress—intelligence, experience, and his rifle. By applying logic and reasoning, he should be able to outsmart her. Also, having hunted tigers for fifteen years, he was knowledgeable of their habits and instincts. Finally, being able to shoot accurately should allow him to kill the tigress before she got close enough to kill him.

With that analysis in mind, he numbered the tigress's advantages. She knew the territory better than Jim, and she was certainly stronger, faster, and larger. She knew how to conceal herself from detection and move through the terrain with considerable stealth. Finally, she was a far more efficient killer in a close encounter. Jim sighed and thought, *This is certainly more difficult than what I had envisioned it would be. When will I get a break?* Just then, he did.

He was just outside the village talking to an Indian official when he saw a man running toward him. "Sahib! The tiger just killed a girl!" the villager yelled from nearly a hundred feet away.

"Quick! Lead me to the location!" Jim shouted as he grabbed his rifle and cartridges.

The excited man had difficulty speaking and running at the same time, so Jim told him to remain quiet. As soon as they entered the village, Jim saw a throng of villagers in a state of panic. He shepherded a man away from the group to ask him what had happened.

The man pointed toward a stand of oak trees on a nearby hill. "A tiger attacked a young girl while she was collecting fodder," he blurted excitedly.

Jim ran to the site and found a pool of fresh blood, a broken bead necklace, and the telltale pug marks of the man-eater. He quickly ascertained which direction the tiger had departed with its victim, and took off in fast pursuit.

As had happened so many times before, the tigress took her kill a considerable distance over rugged terrain. While following her tracks, Jim found bloodstains, strands of the girl's long black hair, and her clothes. Once again, the man-eater was carrying a naked girl, only this time, the tigress's burden was mercifully dead.

Jim tracked the tigress relentlessly, telling himself that this time she was not going to escape. The trail led down a steep hill covered with bamboo and brush to a small stream at the bottom. Jim followed the tracks along the stream for nearly six hundred yards to where it met an adjoining ravine. A small pool lay at the junction, and the tigress had stopped there to feed on the young victim.

In his haste to catch up, Jim's approach had startled the tigress and she'd darted up the embankment with her kill just before he arrived. Jim stared at the pitiful sight next to the pool in disbelief. Blood spatters and bone splinters were scattered about. Part of the girl's leg and foot lay nearby, blood seeping from them into the water. The tigress's pug marks were everywhere, and bloodstained water was seeping into one of the paw prints.

"Water seeping into the paw print!" Jim gasped as he swung his rifle around, pointing the muzzle toward the crest of the embankment. Simultaneously, dislodged dirt and pebbles came rolling down the hill. Jim realized the tigress was at the top, watching his every move. His quick reaction of pointing the rifle uphill had caused the beast to check its attack and run off.

Jim sprinted up the embankment, picked up the man-eater's tracks, and followed them to a desolate wilderness area consisting of treacherous rocky terrain covered with thick brush. Here the going was very slow due to the cracks and chasms between the rocks.

Jim recalled a phrase told to him years ago by another hunter: "When you go out hunting for a tiger, make sure you are prepared to *see* a tiger." Jim had heard stories about hunters who froze in fear when they encountered a tiger in the wild. Nothing can prepare you for the fright and intimidation caused by a charging, enraged tiger. Tigers try to close to within fifty feet before they attack, depending on the availability of concealing terrain, so the prey or hunter has little time to react—only seconds, if that long. To delay pulling the trigger due to fear tips the scales in favor of the tiger, often leaving the hunter fatally mauled.

At several places, Jim saw where the man-eater had rested and continued her meal. At each stop, Jim's approach caused her to pick up the girl's carcass and move to another spot. The grisly sight of blood and bone splinters at each location incensed Jim and encouraged him onward.

Occasionally, he heard the tigress growl her displeasure at having her meal disturbed. Although the sound was terrifying, it provided Jim with the hope that he would be able to finally finish the task he had set out to do. This girl was the man-eater's 436th victim, and Jim was determined to bring the tigress to justice.

However, a glance at the setting sun told Jim that he would have to abandon his pursuit and return to the village. He had been tracking the beast for over four hours, and he was physically and emotionally whipped.

Reluctantly, Jim quietly and carefully exited the area while contemplating his options. He figured the tigress would eat the rest of its victim throughout the night, then rest in the immediate area during the next day. Conducting a beat in the morning might flush her out and give him an opportunity for a shot at her. But persuading the villagers to conduct a beat in this area after all they had been through would be yet another matter! Still, he had to try.

By the time Jim arrived back in Champawat, it was nightfall. When he told the village chief about the situation with the man-eater and his plan to conduct a beat in the morning, the chief was quite receptive to the idea. He indicated he would round up as many men as he could and meet Jim at 10 A.M. near the tree where the young girl had been attacked.

At first light the following morning, Jim went to inspect the area where he intended to conduct the beat. Convinced there was nothing wrong with the idea, he headed back to the village to col-lect whoever had agreed to risk their lives to carry this plan out. He knew how frightened these poor villagers were and how diffi-cult it would be to get them to conduct a beat against a formidable enemy that had killed so many of their friends and family.

When Jim arrived at the tree, the village chief and two other men were the only ones there. Just as Jim was beginning to doubt that the plan would work, other men began showing up in groups of two and three. Men continued to arrive until nearly three hun-dred were present.

Jim could not believe this. When he expressed surprise to the village chief, the man grinned and explained that he had told everyone he would look the other way if anyone brought any unli-censed firearms along with them to the beat. Jim looked at the old relics many had brought and wondered if they would even fire.

Jim escorted the men to the area where he had left the tigress the evening before and explained his strategy. The men were to line up abreast along the crest of the steep ridge surrounding the area where Jim expected the tigress to be. When they saw him wave his handkerchief at the far end of the gorge, they were to fire off their weapons, beat on drums and pots, and shout as loudly as they could. But under no circumstances were they to descend into the valley.

Jim and the village chief left the men on the ridge and proceeded quickly to the far end of the gorge. The chief suspected that many of the weapons the men carried would explode when fired, so he decided to accompany Jim.

Somehow there must have been a miscommunication. Before Jim and the chief arrived at their destination, the men began firing their weapons and making a din. Jim sprinted to the far end of the gorge as fast as he could, nearly stumbling and breaking his neck on numerous occasions.

By the time he'd covered the 150 yards to the gorge, he did not have time to find a good hide. So he crouched down into the two-foot-tall grass and watched intently for the tigress. When the noise from the men on the ridge reached a crescendo, Jim caught sight of the man-eater bounding down a grassy slope about three hundred yards away. The village chief, who was still only halfway down the hill, fired off both barrels of his shotgun at the tigress. The man-eater spun around and headed back to the dense cover from which she'd come. In a flash, Jim raised his rifle and sent a bullet after her, to no avail.

As Jim rammed another cartridge into the empty chamber, the men, believing the tigress had been killed, ended their noisemaking. Jim thought the tigress would scramble her way to the top of the ridge, and held his breath waiting to hear the men start screaming in fright. But just then, the tigress reappeared from the dense cover to Jim's left front, bounded across the stream, and headed for the gorge where Jim was waiting. He raised his rifle and aimed carefully. "All right, Stripes," he whispered, "this is it!"

He squeezed the trigger, listening to the rifle's deafening report. Upon feeling the impact of the bullet, the tiger stopped in its tracks, thirty yards away. Jim shuddered when he realized his rifle had been sighted at sea level and the bullet had hit the tigress farther back than he intended.

The man-eater turned and faced Jim, snarling viciously. Jim aimed quickly and fired again, allowing for the sight differential. The tigress flinched, but did not fall. It bared its teeth and hissed a bloodcurdling sound that signaled an imminent attack.

Jim froze with fear. He had brought only three cartridges with him, believing he would not need any more. Here he was, out of ammunition and face-to-face with the man-eater.

The tigress stood motionless for several seconds, staring at Jim, ears laid back, fangs bared, and growling a guttural sound that frightened Jim to numbness. It was the mortal fear of knowing you are going to die and accepting your fate in petrified silence. Jim closed his eyes, prepared for the inevitable.

When he heard water splashing, he opened his eyes to see the tigress bounding across the stream and returning to the rocky terrain. Just then, Jim found religion. "Oh thank you, God!" he whispered. "Thank you! Thank you, Lord! Thank you!"

Regaining control of his body and faculties, Jim ran to the village chief, snatched the gun from his hands, and went after the tigress. As Jim crossed the stream, the tigress reemerged from the brush to face him. She was standing on a rocky ledge not more than twenty feet in front of Jim.

Jim raised the gun to fire and became horror-stricken to see a gap of nearly three-eighths of an inch between the barrels and the breech-lock. If the gun did not burst when fired, it most certainly could blind Jim by a blowback. Nevertheless, he had no choice. He quickly aligned the sight and fired at the tigress's gaping mouth. Fearing a blowback, he flinched slightly, causing the cylindrical projectile to strike the tigress's front paw. Jim gasped. He knew it would be asking for too much luck to have his skin saved again.

But luck prevailed. Fortunately, the tigress was near her last gasp, and the blow on her foot was enough to cause her to collapse dead on the rock. By this time, the village men were running to the site, shouting, "Hack it to bits! Hack the *shaitan* to pieces!"

Jim managed to scale the ridge to protect the carcass, hoping that the tigress was indeed dead. Like a swarm of locusts, the men descended from all directions, brandishing swords, knives, spears, and axes. Jim understood their rage as he stood guard over the prostrated tigress. Every man present had lost a loved one to the man-eater, and they wanted to exact revenge the only way they knew how.

Eventually, the anger subsided. When Jim thought it safe, he climbed off the rock and instructed the men to fetch the tigress. When the man-eater lay on the ground, Jim walked up and saluted her as a tribute to a brave and worthy adversary.

Jim inspected the tigress, noticing the broken canine teeth caused by a gunshot wound. He shook his head in disgust, knowing that some careless hunter in Nepal had caused all this human misery over the past several years. Jim agreed not to skin the tigress until the men had a chance to carry it through the surrounding villages to prove that their dreaded foe was dead.

When the tigress was lashed to two strong saplings, the crowd began its journey to the villages. Jim headed back to Champawat to prepare for his journey back home and to get some much needed rest. That evening, he skinned the tigress next to a large bonfire with a huge crowd of curious onlookers present.

A policeman was selected to guard the carcass during the night, and the following morning, it was to be cut into small pieces and distributed to the villagers as talismans to give courage and ward off evil. In Jim's opinion, the grit these villagers had exhibited living under the man-eater's dreadful tyranny the past four years was ample proof of their courage. They certainly did not need any amulets!

Although the villagers were preparing a huge festival to honor Jim on the morrow, he had to beg off and begin his long journey back home. Jim said his farewells and rode off pleased, knowing these wonderful people could once again walk throughout the territory without fear.

On his way to Naini Tal, Jim stopped briefly at Pali to show the woman who had been struck dumb the tigress's pelt. Upon seeing the pelt, the woman wept with joy. Miraculously, her voice returned and she went running up and down the street encouraging all who could hear to come see what the sahib had brought. After sharing some tea with the elated villagers, Jim proceeded on his way.

When Jim arrived in Naini Tal two days later, he was greeted by a throng of joyous townfolk. Maggie, who was leading the assembly, threw her arms around Jim's neck and gave him a tight hug. The deputy district commissioner and several other prominent men from the village congratulated Jim with handshakes and slaps on the back. Jim tried to be cordial, but he was dead tired from his strenuous ordeal. He thanked everyone for coming out and greeting him, and told them politely he needed some rest. The crowd followed him back to his house and finally dispersed only when he and Maggie were inside.

As Jim peered out the window, he exclaimed, "Good Lord! I can't believe this!"

"You don't know the half of it," Maggie responded. "The lieutenant-governor is coming here tomorrow to present you with some sort of reward."

"Sir John?"

"Yes. You're a hero now."

"Why? All I did was shoot a tiger!"

"Not just any tiger, but a man-eater. The tiger no one else could kill. Let these British snobs stick that in their bottoms!"

"Maggie!" Jim admonished.

Just then, Mary entered through the back door, her face flushed with excitement. "Jim! Thank God you're all right!" She threw her arms around him and kissed him on the cheek.

"I'm fine . . . "

"You wouldn't believe what happened today," Mary interrupted. "I was invited to the tea on Sunday. Can you believe it? And that's not all. Lady Tennaman actually spoke to me today. Me! Can you believe it? I can't believe it! Oh dear," Mary remarked while heading for her bedroom, "what shall I wear to the tea?"

Jim and Maggie stood staring at each other, then began to laugh.

"What is going on around here?"

"Oh, Jim, ever since the telegram came in yesterday about you shooting the man-eater, this town has been going mad. Two days ago, no one even noticed us. Now it's as though gold was discovered on our veranda. I guess things are going to change for us now, aren't they?"

"I suppose so."

The next day at 2:00 P.M., several of Jim's neighbors came to the house to escort him, Maggie, and Mary to the large, grassy parade grounds next to the deputy commissioner's residence. Jim couldn't believe the multitude of people attending the ceremony. Most of Naini Tal's residents were there, as were many others from outlying areas—British military officers dressed in their formal uniforms, high-ranking government officials, prominent Indian officials, even a military band playing lively tunes!

British and Indian children from the village were playing and running all over the field. Long tables, adorned with ornate cloths and covered with sumptuous food, were located at the center of the grounds.

Jim and his family were led to the section reserved for special guests. They were greeted enthusiastically by men and women anxious to shake Jim's hand and congratulate him for his success. The drummers in the band began a rolling "tappity-tappity-tap" to urge people to take their seats.

No sooner was Jim seated than when Deputy Commissioner Berthoud exited his house accompanied by the lieutenant-governor. Everyone stood and applauded until the lieutenant-governor took the lectern. Sir John Hewett began by welcoming everyone and thanking them for attending. He continued, "Today we are here to honor and congratulate a very courageous man who destroyed the man-eating tiger of Champawat. This man-eater, which had killed over four hundred human beings over the past four years, had successfully eluded the country's best hunters until Jim Corbett took up the challenge. When I was told how he finally defeated his adversary, I was shocked. I know he is too modest to tell you the details, so I will. You know how modest I am." The crowd erupted in laughter.

When order was resumed, Hewett enlightened the audience about Jim's bravery, embellishing the truth as far as was plausible. When he finished, he called Jim to the lectern and presented him with a long, flat box wrapped in green paper with a large white bow. Jim opened the box and couldn't believe his eyes. Inside was a new .275 Rigby rifle with Jim's name inscribed on a plate attached to the carved solid walnut stock. Jim was shocked. He looked over at Mary and Maggie and saw the pride beaming from their faces. He didn't even hear the standing ovation from the crowd.

Hewett leaned toward Jim and whispered, "There's plenty of ammunition that goes with the rifle."

Jim shook Hewett's hand, then made a short speech thanking everyone for their kindness. When he was through, Hewett took the lectern again and remarked, "Before we adjourn to the drinks and delicious food, I wish to pose a question to the audience." There was laughter, followed by silence. "I'm sure most of you have heard about the man-eater in the Panar area that has killed numerous people over the past year and a half. Do you think it's time that Jim takes a crack at it?"

The crowd roared its approval and applauded. Jim was speechless. He looked over at Hewett, who was smiling slyly. He glanced at Mary and Maggie and noticed the concern in their eyes. He then looked at the crowd, which was cheering and shouting his name.

Jim did not want to accept this challenge, but he knew he had to. Mary and Maggie were reveling in their new social status. Life for them would never be the same again. Hunting was "king" in India, and Jim was now carrying the scepter. He was fearful that he would not be able to live up to everyone's expectations. He now realized that fame carries a price. Whenever other hunters were unable to destroy a man-eater, people would look to him for resolution. Unfortunately, by then the man-eater would be wise to all the common tricks used to entrap it. Jim would have to find new and more dangerous techniques, which would place his life in greater jeopardy.

Jim raised his new rifle above his head and shouted, "I'll do it!"

As the crowd roared its approval, Jim looked over at Sir John. He was smiling broadly, pleased with the satisfaction of accomplishing his mission. As he shook Jim's hand, he commented, "Our government and the people truly appreciate what you are doing. Good luck!"

There was no turning back. Jim only hoped the frequency of man-eaters would be minimal. He was to be proved wrong.

14

The wedding ceremony was perfect—gorgeous weather, stunningly beautiful bride and handsome groom, 256 guests, and an abundance of sumptuous food and drinks. Kyle and Beth beamed when the minister announced them husband and wife, sealing their bond with a tender kiss.

Jim was ecstatic that his best friend was finally settling down with his childhood sweetheart. Kyle and Beth had become inseparable since Kyle was fifteen. They'd had their share of disagreements, but everyone knew they were made for each other and would eventually wed. Even though Jim often felt like the odd man out, Kyle insisted Jim accompany him and Beth whenever possible. So Jim went . . . because he and Kyle were the best of friends. Beth felt a little uneasy at first about their threesome, but she eventually accepted Jim as her best friend too. Whenever Kyle and Beth quarreled, it was always Jim who intervened and got their relationship back on track.

Jim's friendship with the two of them meant the world to him, and it was his love of both of them that kept his crush on Beth at bay. Besides, Jim had found his real love, a love that never went away—the hunt. Except for Punatii and Sarah, Jim had a hard time being a ladies' man. He was grand when he hunted, but quite shy one-on-one. Kyle was the bold one—the one who was handsome, gregarious, and outgoing. He always felt at ease with girls, and always tried to pull Jim out of his shell. Whenever a girl approached, Jim remained cool and silent to mask his inability to converse. In fact, it took a long time before Jim could chat in a normal manner with Beth without feeling awkward.

Jim took a week off from work to attend Kyle's wedding. He stood next to a long linen-covered table, indulging in food that he had missed so much while away at work.

"Aren't you going to kiss the bride?"

Jim spun around to see Beth smiling radiantly in her white wedding gown.

"Of course," he said, and leaned into her.

He felt a tingling in his head and lips, but quickly dodged the feeling.

"Ease up there, ol' chap," Kyle laughed as he pulled Jim back. "I saw her first."

"Lucky for you!" Jim smiled and playfully punched Kyle on the shoulder.

"We need to get going, darling, if we're going to catch our ship," Kyle said, kissing Beth's lacy, gloved hand.

Kyle and Beth had arranged to honeymoon in Africa. One of Beth's uncles was a game warden in Kenya and had invited them to stay with him on several occasions. Kyle had always wanted to hunt big game in Africa and elected to take advantage of the invitation upon marrying Beth.

"Sure you don't want to join us, Jim?" Kyle asked sincerely. "Beth's uncle has plenty of room, and you could stay as long as you like."

Jim was unsure how to react. He would have loved to go to Africa to hunt, but he felt strange tagging along on his friend's honeymoon, especially considering he had hidden feelings for Beth. He felt terribly guilty, but truly wanted to join them.

"For heaven's sake, Kyle, this is your honeymoon!" he finally said. "You don't want some oaf tagging along and ruining it for you."

"Jim, I'm serious as cobra's venom. You've always been our best friend, and we'd love to have you along."

Beth placed her tiny hand on Jim's arm and added, "You know I feel the same as Kyle. Why don't you come?"

"I can't. Not that I don't want to, but I have to return to my job."

"Damnation, Jim, I wish you'd quit that job. We hardly see you anymore, and I know your mother and Maggie want you here in Naini Tal."

"It's just for another few years. As soon as I can find someone to replace me, I'll come back."

"Replacement? Who the blazes would want that job besides you?"

Beth tugged at Kyle's sleeve. "Come on, Kyle. We need to get to the railway station."

Kyle looked at Beth. "You're right. Well Jim, this is goodbye for a couple months. See you when we return."

Jim shook Kyle's hand and helped Beth into the waiting buggy. He waved as Kyle's father slapped the horse with the reins.

"Have a good time!" Jim called out.

The knot in Jim's stomach subsided the farther away they got, and he wiped the sweat from his brow. *Thank goodness*, he thought. Just then, Percy Wyndham walked up to Jim. He had recently been appointed deputy commissioner at Naini Tal and was known to be very ambitious.

"I don't think I've had the pleasure," Wyndham announced as he extended his sweaty, chubby hand.

At age fifty-two, he was portly and sported thinning white hair. Everyone knew he aspired to become governor of the United Provinces and saw this posting as a steppingstone to achieving his goal. Wyndham was first and foremost a politician, and gauged all his decisions by how they would ultimately affect his career. Thus he was slow to make decisions but quick to ingratiate himself with any dignitary who visited Naini Tal.

"You must be the new deputy commissioner," Jim replied graciously "I'm Ji . . . "

"Mister Corbett," Wyndham interrupted, smiling broadly. "Yes, I know. Your reputation as a hunter is well known throughout the United Provinces."

Jim was surprised the deputy commissioner knew him.

"Actually, I was talking to your mother and sister a few minutes ago, and they pointed you out to me. I wanted to meet you before you return to Bengal."

"Oh . . . why?"

"You've no doubt heard that the frequency of man-eaters throughout the provinces has increased substantially. Our adjoining districts are having the same problem we're having, and the district commissioners have solicited the governor's assistance. Sir John, in turn, has asked me to request your help in this regard."

"I'm honored, but I don't know if I'll have the time. My job has been very demanding, and it's becoming more difficult for me to take time off."

"We know that, Mister Corbett, and the governor and I will be happy to intervene with your supervisor so you can tend to these man-eaters. Right now, these beasts are our top priority. Many people are getting killed by them, and the people look to us for resolution. If we sit on our hands too long, they may start rioting."

"I had no idea it was becoming so ser . . . "

"Yes, it's very serious. We'll continue to deputize other hunters first, as we have in the past. But to be quite frank, most of them lack the will or expertise for this type of mission. If they fail, as many have already, we'll have no choice but to ask for your help."

Wyndham and Jim stood silent for several seconds, staring at each other.

"Your government needs you, Jim. May I call you Jim? Your success at destroying these man-eaters helps quiet the voices who criticize our government and attempt to stir up trouble."

"I'll most certainly be glad to help, provided you can persuade my boss to release me."

"That will be no problem, I assure you. Well, I know you want to spend more time with your mother and sister before you have to return to Bengal, so I won't keep you any longer. Incidentally, you may be receiving a wire from me in a couple of months."

"Oh? Why is that?"

"A man-eating tiger in the Ladhya Valley region near Nepal has killed over forty people. There are three hunters there now trying to put an end to the carnage. I hope they succeed, but if they don't, you'll be hearing from me."

"I see," said Jim as he shook Wyndham's hand. "It was a pleasure meeting you."

" . . . and you too, Jim."

As Wyndham walked away, Jim glanced over at his mother and Maggie. They appeared to be having a great time socializing with the other women, so Jim took this opportunity to escape back to the house. As he stepped onto the porch, a neighbor ran up to the house.

"Sahib!" Ram gasped. "The leopard just killed another one of my cattle."

There was a large male leopard in the area that had been taking several of his neighbors' livestock and destroying their livelihood. Ram asked Jim to rid them of this pest, and Jim accepted the challenge. He quickly donned his hunting clothes, grabbed his rifle and ammunition, and followed Ram to the scene of the attack.

Jim thought it unusual that the leopard had struck in broad daylight. These animals normally stalk their prey during the cover of darkness. However, this particular leopard was known for its boldness and, unless stopped, would cause considerable hardship to these poor villagers. Ram's house was at the edge of the village, not too far from the forest. This location made it easier for him to herd his cattle into the forest for grazing, but it also made his cattle prime targets for any marauders.

When Jim and Ram arrived at the attack site, Jim quickly analyzed the pug marks. Splashes of crimson blood punctuated the ground, and the grassy turf was torn up extensively where the cow had made its last stand.

"It's him, all right!" Jim announced as he ran his fingers over the pug marks. Drag marks in the dirt made by the cow's hind legs were prominently displayed next to the leopard's prints.

"Stay here, Ram. I must track it alone."

"Yes, Sahib." Though disappointed, Ram understood Jim's reasons for hunting alone—stealth and safety. Nothing is more dangerous than hunting with an anxiety-ridden companion with a nervous trigger finger.

Jim followed the trail into the forest, hoping he could locate the thief before nightfall. Two hours of daylight remained. The leopard's boldness kept playing in Jim's mind as he followed the trail up and down the forested hills. To date, the cat's only offense was killing livestock. However, it was likely only a matter of time before it added humans to its diet.

As Jim approached a small stream winding through a deep ravine, he heard a growl. He dropped to his knees and listened intently, trying to determine the direction of the noise. Shadows from the trees were creeping toward the east, obscuring his vision. He waited silently, listening to the forest. Everything appeared normal.

Jim rose to his feet and moved on. The drag and blood trail led down to the stream, which was bordered by thick bushes. When he reached the stream, he noticed an object protruding from the bushes to his front. Waning daylight made it difficult to see clearly, so Jim released the safety on his rifle and crept closer to the object. When he was within forty feet, he realized it was the hind leg of a cow. He scanned the immediate area for the leopard, but it was gone.

*Damn!* he muttered to himself, realizing that the leopard had seen or heard him coming and abandoned its kill.

Because dusk was fast approaching, Jim had to make a decision. He could either return to Naini Tal and give up his pursuit, or sit up over the kill for a while and hope the leopard would return. The cow's carcass was still intact, so there was a good chance the leopard would come back for a meal.

Jim surveyed the surrounding area and selected a large oak tree protruding from the side of the hill as a good place to wait. He cleared the brush from around the carcass to give him a better field of fire, then climbed into the oak. He hoped the ordeal would be finished within the next couple of hours so he could return home and prepare for his journey to Bengal the next evening.

Jim found a large branch twenty feet from the ground that provided suitable comfort. He straddled the branch with his legs and rested his back against the trunk. He closed his eyes and listened to the forest, as Kunwah had taught him many years before. Everything appeared normal.

The night was cool, and the wind increased, causing a suspicious movement of shadows in the silver moonlight. The moon was approximately half full, but thin cloud cover made visibility difficult. One hour later, with the forest at peace, Jim dozed off.

Near midnight, Jim was abruptly wakened by an unusual sound. When his eyes focused, he saw the cow still lying in the same position. He heard a faint noise again, and a sharp chill ran throughout his body. The leopard was present, and it was behind him.

A low, sinister growl erupted from under the tree, and Jim heard the scratching sound from the leopard's claws as it began ascending the tree on the opposite side. Jim cursed his inability to maneuver around in his seat, which would have enabled him to see behind him. He began shouting as loudly as he could in an attempt to startle the leopard, hoping it would leave. The leopard was not known to be a man-eater, so Jim wanted it to realize there was a human in the tree.

After yelling at the top of his lungs, he listened intently. Deathly silence. After what seemed an eternity, Jim heard the scratching noise again—coming closer. Perspiration was flowing from every pore in his body, and he was seized by a sudden spell of dizziness.

Out of options, Jim realized he had but one chance to save his life. Slowly but deliberately, he swung his rifle around so the barrel was pointing down toward the ground at a forty-five-degree angle and as far behind him as he could possibly reach. To accomplish this feat, he could use only one arm, which caused a painful strain. Seconds later, he felt pressure against the barrel, and discharged the rifle. The leopard screamed in agony, followed by the sounds of branches snapping and a distinct thud at the bottom of the tree. Jim quickly rammed another shell into the chamber while listening for the cat. Nothing stirred.

Clouds completely covered the moon now, leaving Jim with insufficient light to detect anything or any movement below him. His only recourse was to remain in the tree until daylight. The remaining four hours of darkness were the most stressful wait that Jim had ever encountered. Throughout the remainder of the night, he continued to look down at the base of the tree for the leopard and listen for any sounds.

Finally, at daybreak, he was able to make out the shape of the large cat lying approximately five feet from the tree. When sufficient light permitted an accurate aim, Jim sent a bullet crashing into the leopard's skull. The animal never flinched. Slowly, Jim lowered himself from the tree.

The leopard was a magnificent male in the prime of life. Upon further inspection, Jim noticed an old gunshot wound in its right shoulder that had incapacitated the animal to the extent that it was unable to catch its normal prey. The hunter who had shot the leopard had failed to follow up and destroy it, resulting in its preying on livestock. There was no doubt in Jim's mind that the animal eventually would have added humans to its diet. If he had not destroyed it, he probably would have become the leopard's first human victim.

Two hours later, Jim had the leopard's pelt rolled up and tucked away in his mesh bag and was heading for home. On the way to his house, he stopped and informed Ram that he wouldn't be troubled by the leopard anymore. At home, Jim found an anxious mother and sister waiting for him.

"Jim!" shouted Mary. "Where have you been? We've been at wit's end thinking something dreadful had happened."

"Sorry, Mum," Jim replied earnestly. "I had the opportunity to destroy the leopard that had been killing all the livestock around here lately, and I couldn't pass it up. I never intended to stay out all night, but it was the only option I had."

"I only wish you would have left a note or told someone," Mary admonished as she kissed Jim's cheek. "I have to help some new tenants move into the Johnson residence. Maggie will help you pack. Have a safe trip back," Mary yelled as she rushed out the door.

"Let me see the pelt!" Maggie cried in excitement.

15

O ver the next year and a half, the Ladhya Valley man-eater's notoriety increased immeasurably. When Jim returned home for a holiday in October 1912, government had attributed fifty-seven known deaths to the man-eater. Numerous others who had been mauled by the tiger and had eventually died were not counted among the toll.

Jim sat across the large, polished oak desk from Percy Wyndham, listening intently to the circumstances surrounding the man-eater's reign of terror and the attempts to destroy it.

"Christ!" Wyndham said, obviously annoyed. "Three British hunters, two of them officers, are included in the death toll. The government has increased the bounty five times—up to 500 rupees—and still no one has been able to kill that demon. This is just preposterous!"

"If you want me to take a crack at it, just say so," Jim sighed, knowing Wyndham's tact.

Wyndham leaned forward in his chair and stared into Jim's eyes. "I want you to take a crack at it." He puffed on his pipe. "But there are complications."

"What complications?"

"I promised Kyle that he could try first."

"What? Kyle is married—has responsibilities. He can't do this!"

"Sorry, Jim," Wyndham said sheepishly. "I am under enormous pressure to resolve this, and was running out of options. You hadn't volunteered, so I accepted Kyle's offer." Wyndham's face took on a stern look. "I had no choice!"

Jim grabbed his hat and stood up. "Yes, you did, damn it! You could have denied the request. You should have wired me."

Wyndham sighed. "It wouldn't have made any difference. His mind was made up, and he would've gone over my head if I had turned him down."

As Jim exited Wyndham's office, he realized Wyndham was right. Kyle's uncle had close personal connections with the governor and the viceroy, and Kyle would have used that trump card if necessary. "Damn you, Kyle!" Jim mumbled to himself as he walked briskly to Kyle's house. "You bloody fool!"

Jim ran up the steps to the porch and pounded on the front door. Seconds later, it was opened.

"Sahib," the male Indian servant acknowledged. "Benton Sahib went to the railway station."

"He's already gone?" Jim shouted as he grabbed the servant's shoulders.

"Yes, Sahib, to hunt the tiger."

Jim sprinted home, saddled and jumped onto his mare, and galloped off to the station. Forty minutes later, as he pulled up to the hitching post, he noticed Kyle and Beth standing on the loading platform. He jumped from the mare and bolted toward his friend.

"Kyle! What do you think you're doing?"

"Jim!" Kyle replied, surprised to see him. "I didn't know you were home."

"Just arrived," panted Jim. "Tell me, you're not going after that tiger in the Ladhya Valley, are you?"

Kyle remained quiet, staring at Jim. Jim turned to look at Beth and saw the fear in her eyes.

"Damn you, Kyle," Jim blurted as he turned back toward his friend. "So you are going. You must be mad!"

"Afraid of a little competition, ol' chum?" Kyle had a strange look in his eyes.

"What on earth do you mean?"

"I would also like to receive recognition for my hunting skills. You have already been feted for destroying three man-eaters. I've decided to prove to everyone that I can kill these animals too."

"That's preposterous! You don't need to prove anything. Everyone already knows how good a hunter you are."

"I have to do it for myself, dammit!"

Jim understood the futility of arguing with Kyle. He looked at Beth for help.

"Don't waste your breath, Jim," Beth sighed. "You know how stubborn he can be."

Jim looked back at Kyle. "Let me go with you then. We'll hunt it together." Jim bit his tongue, trying desperately not to say anything that would upset Beth more than she already was.

Kyle shook his head. "I have to do this alone."

"Please reconsider, Kyle." Jim wanted to grab Kyle by the lapels of his khaki hunting jacket and shake some sense into him. He wanted to tell him how dangerous this was; how foolish he was to undertake such a venture. He wanted to, but he couldn't—not with Beth standing next to them.

"My mind's made up, Jim." Kyle glanced toward the dirty passenger coach to watch his servants load his gear. "Be careful with that!" he yelled as they struggled with a heavy canvas bag. He turned back and put his hand on Jim's shoulder. "Look after Beth while I'm gone, will you?"

"Of course," Jim acknowledged as he shook Kyle's hand. "How long do you think you'll be away?"

"One month, no more. I need to be back for Beth's birthday." He smiled at Beth and nudged her. She clutched his arm and looked thoughtfully into his eyes.

Jim stood fast as Beth walked Kyle to his compartment. They stopped in front of the door, and Kyle reached for her, pulling her in tight. He kissed her gently on the cheek and, with a wave of his hat, boarded the train. When the engine pulled out, Jim took Beth's arm and walked her toward her carriage, where Beth struggled to put on a brave face.

"Kyle is such a mule!" she forced herself to laugh. "I can't understand why he is so keen on doing this."

She peeked up at Jim to see if he would play along. He saw the fear reflected in her emerald eyes, so he decided that he would.

"Don't worry, Kyle's a good hunter. He can take care of himself—and that big cat too."

Beth nodded slightly, wanting to believe. Jim wanted to believe too.

"Just think how grand it will all be when he comes home— 'the country's hero'! It will be impossible to contain him!"

Beth sighed and again forced a smile, then boarded her coach. Once seated, she looked at Jim from the window. He could see the tears welling up in her eyes, and it stuck a lump in his throat.

The servant slapped the reins, and Beth was gone. Jim stood for a moment, watching her go. *What a damn lucky man*, he thought. Beth was the kind of woman all men dream of, all men want to come home to—all men except cat hunters, he reminded himself as he walked on.

On his ride back to town, Jim's thoughts were consumed by his reckless friend and the dangerous mission on which he had embarked. Kyle had always been lucky, though, no one could deny that. Born to a prominent family, he was never at want for anything. He had it all—charm, intelligence, personality, good looks, and money. Fiercely competitive, he had to be the best at every-thing. He envied Jim's sudden fame when he'd destroyed the Champawat, Muktesar, and Panar man-eaters. When Kyle was subjected to the snide, cutting remarks made by others at the pub about his mettle, that was the final straw: He knew he had to do something to restore his pride and self-esteem. What better proof than to destroy the man-eater no one else had been able to for the past two years?

Kyle and his servants arrived in the small village of Sem with-out incident, two days after departing Naini Tal. He was met at the train station by several members of the village, who assisted Kyle to an abandoned hut that would serve as his base of operations while in pursuit of the man-eater. The woman who had been attacked on 9 October was the man-eater's fifty-seventh victim. Several attempts made by other hunters to end the man-eater's reign of terror had failed, and the cunning tiger had achieved considerable reputation for its elusiveness and ferocity.

On the morning of 14 October, a man from Kot Kindri, a nearby village, traveled to Sem as quickly as he could to notify Kyle of a tragedy that had occurred the preceding afternoon. The exhausted villager indicated that a man had been attacked and killed by a tiger just before sunset in a cultivated field near his village. This was the opportunity Kyle was waiting for. He ordered his men to assemble his gear, and they quickly made their trek to Kot Kindri.

Kyle and his entourage arrived at midafternoon and, following a quick meal while determining the exact location of the attack, set off to track the big cat. Next to a large tree approximately sixty yards from the edge of the village, Kyle found a large splash of dried blood where the unfortunate villager had met his fate. The ground was damp and soft, making it easy for Kyle to determine which way the tiger had dragged its victim. The drag marks left the trail about thirty feet beyond the tree and proceeded up a steep hill covered with thick foliage. Tracking was slow due to the heavily forested route along which the tiger had taken its kill.

Two hours later, after Kyle had traveled approximately one and a half miles, he noticed the drag marks led down into a ravine containing a dense thicket. Beyond the thicket was a rocky cliff that was too steep for anything to climb. The man-eater had cornered itself, leaving only one way out.

When Kyle stepped across the stream that ran through the ravine, he heard the angry growl of the tiger. Assuming the growl was only a warning, he approached the thicket cautiously.

Kyle signaled his men to begin throwing stones into the thicket, hoping to startle the tiger and permit him to get a shot while it attempted an escape. As the first stone was on its way, Kyle raised his rifle and pointed it toward the area where he expected the tiger to be.

"This is too easy," Kyle chuckled to himself as he watched the hurled stone soaring to its destination. He tightened his grip on his rifle, anxious to put an end to the man-eater's reign of terror. He could visualize the look of envy among his peers when the governor feted him for his accomplishment. How proud Beth would be!

However, in his haste to end the hunt quickly, Kyle failed to notice the sudden change in wind direction. Nor did he detect the leaves on the bush to his immediate left agitate ever so slightly.

"AAOORRR!" The tiger charged from the thicket to Kyle's left, its huge paws kicking up a cloud of dust. Kyle saw the tawny beast from the corner of his eye and realized he had been outmaneuvered. With only a second to react, he dropped to his knees while swinging his rifle around to meet the charging man-killer.

The tiger was quicker. The powerful cat was already launched, its eyes focused on Kyle's vulnerable neck. Kyle realized he was not going to have his rifle in position in time.

"NOOOOOO!" he screamed as the five-hundred-pound beast smashed against his body and flesh-piercing fangs ripped open his throat. He felt agonizing pain shoot into his brain as he was thrust backward. Four-inch, razor-sharp claws gouged Kyle's chest and shoulder. The tiger's massive weight restrained Kyle's movement except for his right leg, which was quivering uncontrollably.

While attempting to flee, one of the men tripped over the tiger and let out an ear-piercing scream while regaining his footing. The ensuing commotion startled the tiger into releasing its hold. Confused, the cat turned toward the fleeing man, roared menacingly, and then fled into the forest.

As soon as the men regained their composure, they returned cautiously to Kyle's severely mauled and bloodied body. They quickly constructed a litter from two thick bamboo poles and some clothing, and carried Kyle back to the village. Mortally wounded, however, Kyle was dead by the time his torn and mutilated body arrived at Sem.

That evening at 7 P.M., Jim was summoned to Wyndham's office. He couldn't help but notice the look of despair on Wyndham's face when he sat down in front of the massive desk.

"Kyle was attacked by the man-eater. He was killed."

Jim's eyes glazed with tears. He clenched his fist until the knuckles were white. "No . . . dammit, no!" he said under his breath.

Jim sat listening to the details of his friend's demise. When Wyndham finished, they both sat in silence for a long while. Jim held his hat in his lap, digging his fingernails in along the brim.

"Would you please cancel the bounty on the man-eater, and order all other hunters out of the Ladhya Valley area?"

"Sure, Jim." Wyndham puffed on his pipe. "There are no other hunters up there, to my knowledge. Everyone has given up, or has been killed."

Jim nodded, still in a state of denial.

"By the way," Wyndham added, "I thought you should be the one to inform Beth. You were so close to them both."

Jim nodded as he headed for the door. "I'll be traveling to Sem tomorrow."

"I'll cancel the bounty immediately. Good luck."

Jim stood outside Wyndham's office momentarily, wondering how, or what, he was going to tell Beth. He gazed down the dusty, hardened dirt road, knowing the three hundred yards to Beth's house would be the most difficult journey of his life. Jim hated being the messenger of bad news. He'd never handled it well. He thought of the village woman at Champawat who had crumpled at his feet and wailed when he brought her the remains of her husband. She had wrapped her arms around his ankles and would not let go. He was so embarrassed, and so heartsick for her, he didn't know what to do. Finally, some of the village men had to pry the woman's arms off and take her away to her house.

Jim knocked on Beth's door just as the amber glow of the setting sun died out. He could hear her quick, short steps as she came toward the door, and then slowly it opened.

"Oh, Jim! Come in!" she said, genuinely pleased to have company. "Take a seat in the parlor, and I'll be right in—I'm just boiling some tea."

Jim wandered into the parlor, his mind reeling with how to break the news to her. Beth called from the kitchen, "Have you had dinner?"

Jim didn't answer—he couldn't. Beth came to the doorway with a cup of tea in her hand.

"Hey," she said sort of smiling, "didn't you hear me?"

Jim looked up. His faced was grim, and it registered on her.

"What is it?" she said, concern resonating in her voice.

Jim stood. "Beth, I don't know how to. . . .

Beth froze, her eyes wild. "It's Kyle, isn't it?" she said, the teacup in her hand beginning to quiver.

Jim nodded, keeping his eyes on her in case she swooned to faint.

"He's dead."

Beth just stood there, a slight tremble growing in her hands that traveled up her torso and to her firmly pursed lips. Suddenly she smashed the teacup to the ground and bolted into the kitchen. Jim followed close behind. She ran for the stove and reached out for the steaming kettle. Her hand gripped the red-hot handle, but no cries came. Jim quickly snatched her hand away and spun her around into him. He held her tight. Beth shook silently, uncontrollably. Then, finally, came the tears. Jim held her. It was all he knew how to do—it was all he *could* do.

After a while he walked her to the couch and they sat. She laid her head on his shoulder and dozed off, completely exhausted. Jim could smell the lilac in her hair. He wondered where she had gotten it—how she always managed to stay so beautiful and bright, even in the raging heat, even in the face of tragedy. His heart began to beat faster. Beth awoke and looked up at him.

"What do we do now?" she said, wiping her swollen eyes.

A million things flashed through Jim's mind. He looked into Beth's face, a face he had seen at night while on the hunt, just before he fell asleep; a face that had comforted and inspired him. Most of all, he saw the face of his dead friend's wife. Jim got up.

"I don't know. I'm too wiped-out to even think," he said as he moved toward the door and opened it. "Will you be all right?"

Beth looked so small, so alone. She nodded faintly. "As all right as I can be, I suppose."

She walked toward him and kissed him on the cheek. "You'll be by tomorrow then?" she said.

"First thing."

Jim turned, and Beth closed the door behind him. He sighed deeply and just stood looking out into the darkness. His head hurt and his eyes burned. He fought the urge to turn around and walk back in. He almost did, but then in the distance he heard several children playing, yelling "Tiger! Tiger!" and the scuffle of bare feet and laughter. The knot in his throat instantly subsided. He wiped his face off, straightened his hat, and strode off toward home, knowing exactly what he needed to do.

It was just before sunup when Jim entered the kitchen to find Maggie preparing breakfast. The sadness in her eyes revealed she had heard the news of Kyle's death.

"Jim," she whispered as she touched his arm, "I'm so sorry about Kyle."

Jim could only nod, afraid he was going to break down over the loss of his best friend. Maggie understood his sorrow. "Sit down. I just made some hot tea."

Mary was in the next room dressing, and Jim did not want to face her—not today.

"I'm going to the Ladhya Valley for a while," Jim announced to Maggie. She stood at the kitchen table slicing a tomato, and the knife slipped off the vegetable and into her finger when she heard the word "Ladhya." Blood trickled from the cut. She turned to face Jim as she pressed a clean cloth over the wound. " . . . the tiger? Oh, Jim, don't!"

"I have to!" Jim seethed as he slammed his fist on the table. "I should've killed it long ago, but I was hoping someone else would destroy it. Now look what my foot-dragging has caused. The death of my best friend!"

Jim rose to his feet and stormed from the kitchen and out the front door. Maggie stood staring at the now-empty doorway with an expression of dismay on her face.

Jim ran to Mothi Singh's house, only a few minutes away. Mothi had accompanied Jim during his previous hunts, and Jim needed him on this quest also. Mothi, of course, jumped at the chance. Not only did Jim pay well, but these hunts also offered a little excitement in his humdrum life. After Jim's success with the Champawat, Muktesar, and Panar man-eaters, Mothi's confidence in Jim's hunting prowess had grown immeasurably. Mothi believed Jim was a *sadhu,* a sacred person with special powers that protected him from danger. Mothi believed nothing bad could ever happen to him when he was with Jim.

When Jim returned to his house, Mary had already departed to visit an ailing neighbor. Maggie was busy cleaning up breakfast, so Jim sneaked into his room to pack his gear. Provisions packed, Jim headed for the door. Mothi would be waiting by the carriage, anxious to go.

"Aren't you going to say good-bye?" Maggie asked as she poked her head through the kitchen doorway.

"I, uh, was hoping to avoid any unpleasantries."

"Is it unpleasant to say good-bye to your sister before you leave on a suicidal trip?"

"Please, Maggie. . . . "

Maggie walked up to Jim and gave him a big hug. "Listen Mister Sahib, you've been doing stupid things all your life, and I've always understood. Why should this time be any different? What will I tell Mother?"

"Tell her I've gone on a hunting journey for a couple of weeks. I don't care. Tell her I need some time away from Naini Tal to get over Kyle. You'll think of something. You always do."

"If Mother only knew about some of the chances you take, it would give her a stroke."

"Would you mind looking in on Beth, to see if she needs anything?"

"Of course not. I plan to visit her this afternoon. What should I tell her about you missing Kyle's funeral?"

" . . . that I had to go away for a while. I just can't attend the funeral, considering what's happened."

"All right, then. You'd better hurry or you'll miss your train."

Jim kissed Maggie on the forehead and pushed open the door.

"Jim!" Maggie yelled as he walked down the road. Jim turned. "Do be careful." Jim nodded, turned, and continued walking.

**16**

Jim and Mothi boarded the train to Tanakpur and were comfortably seated for the eighteen-hour trip. Listening to the coach's wheels going *clickety-clack, clickety-clack* along the rails made Jim drowsy. He had been under extreme emotional stress for the previous two days, and it was taking its toll. He leaned his head against his rolled-up jacket, which he'd wedged between the wooden seat back and the side of the coach, and fell asleep.

When Jim awoke, he gazed out the window to view the passing scenery. They were rolling through the *terai*, an open grassland just south of the foothills. The jade green grass stood out in stark contrast against the snowcapped Himalayan peaks in the distance and the bright blue sky beyond. Fed by crystalline mountain streams, the *terai* was home to many wild animals—elephants, crocodiles, herds of deer, and too many species of birds to catalog.

Directly skirting the *terai* to the north were the forested foothills of the Himalayas—home of tigers and leopards and the many animals on which they prey.

Jim looked over at Mothi. Born and raised in the mountainous Almora District to the north, Mothi was an expert tracker. His skin was dark, even for an Almora native, who were notorious for dark skin. Mothi's wrinkled face and several missing teeth belied his youthful exuberance. Three of his front teeth were gone, and his "toothless" smile could disarm all but the most recalcitrant person.

Although short in stature, Mothi could trek eighteen miles a day with little difficulty, up and down hilly and forested terrain, carrying a heavy pack. He was as knowledgeable of the forest and its inhabitants as Jim, and was extremely proud to be Jim's "right-hand man." In fact, both shared a strong mutual respect and loyalty.

On a hunt, Jim relied heavily on Mothi's advice and assistance, while Mothi depended on Jim's courage and marksmanship. They had formed a powerful bond between them, similar to two soldiers in battle.

Jim was met by the Sem Village headman when they arrived at the train station at Tanakpur.

"Welcome, Sahib! We are most happy you come." The headman's sincerity was obvious. He quickly instructed the other three village men to unload Jim's equipment from the train and place it onto the horse-drawn cart. Then he continued in broken English. "People very frightened. Can not go out from house. Tiger kill too many. You help us, please? You kill demon."

"I'll try," Jim responded in earnest.

Following the seventeen-mile trek on horseback to Sem Village, Jim was offered the use of a small hut provided by the villagers. When he arrived in Sem, he quickly noticed the abject fear on the villagers' faces. Several houses had been vacated by distressed families who had departed the area until the man-eater could be brought to book.

There was not anyone in Sem or the surrounding villages who had not lost a close friend or relative to the tiger. With the help of the village headman, Mothi enlisted six villagers to accompany Jim and him while they were in pursuit of the man-eater. These men were needed to haul Jim's tent and equipment throughout the area as well as to cook, clean, and perform the myriad other necessary tasks that must be accomplished on a day-to-day basis.

While making his acquaintance throughout the village, Jim was introduced to an elderly woman who had lost her husband and only son to the man-eater. When told that Jim was going to hunt the tiger, the woman bent down and touched his feet, making him feel like an impostor.

Most people in India, being devout followers of the Hindu religion, cremate their dead and float the ashes down one of the tributary rivers that flow into the Ganges River. To ensure that the departed reach their heavenly destination, the body or some part of it is needed to perform the ritual. Therefore, every attempt was made to obtain the remains of the deceased, even if he or she had fallen victim to a man-eater. Although Jim supported their religious beliefs, he found it extremely distasteful to return a mauled, half-eaten corpse to the mourning relatives. Having seen the denuded, partially eaten remains of some victims that would make a stone cry, Jim wondered how the families and relatives of these victims could possibly cope.

The fear and intimidation caused by the man-eater's presence were certainly exacting a toll on the villagers. Many were reluctant to leave their huts day or night, and the sanitary conditions were abhorrent. When it was absolutely necessary to move about—to go to market for food or attend to their livestock—several individuals would muster enough courage to accomplish the task collectively.

Jim could only imagine the courage it took to live under a man-eater's tyranny for an extended period of time. He recalled an incident in Mohan Village involving a villager and his son who fell victim to a man-eater. The boy was cutting grass for the livestock when the tiger approached silently from behind, grabbed the boy by the throat, then dragged him into the nearby forest. Later that day, when the boy had not returned home, the father went from house to house inquiring if anyone knew what had happened to his son. Fearing that the boy was seriously injured, the father lit a torch and traveled along the forested paths surrounding the village throughout the night, calling for his son. Knowing that the man-eater had been active in this area did not deter him from his quest. It was discovered later, when they found the boy's remains, that the father had passed within only a few feet of where the tiger was sitting up eating his son.

It had been four days since the last reported attack of the man-eater, so Jim decided to wait at Sem until he heard more news of its location. Everyone in the vicinity was now aware of Jim's presence at Sem and his intent to kill the man-eater. Couriers and *cooee* calls were highly reliable means of communication among the villages.

That afternoon, a *cooee* call relayed from adjacent Chuka Village informed them that a tiger attack had occurred near Kot Kindri Village during late morning. Kot Kindri was six miles directly west of Sem in a heavily forested and mountainous region where elevations exceeded nine thousand feet. The Ladhya River flowed next to the village, having cut a deep ravine through the area.

Jim immediately instructed Mothi to prepare for their journey to Kot Kindri, grabbed his rifle and ammunition, and quickly departed. Although he remained alert en route, Jim was able to cover the distance in three hours. He knew he did not have to worry about being attacked as long as the tiger was preoccupied with its latest kill.

At Kot Kindri, Jim found the villagers in a state of terror and shock. When calm was somewhat restored, the village headman spoke. "Sahib, a tiger killed a girl over there when she carry the water to her house." He was pointing to the edge of the village.

"Can you show me the location of the attack?"

"Yes, Sahib. Come!"

Jim was escorted to the site, and by analyzing bloodstains, pug marks, and drag marks was able to determine the direction the tiger had carried its victim. "Big tiger!" Mothi remarked as he ran his fingers over a paw imprint in the mud. The pug marks were the largest Jim had ever seen, and the toes were splayed significantly, indicating the tiger was either old or of huge proportions. This corresponded with information learned from others concerning the man-eater. Instructing Mothi to set up camp in the village, Jim took off in pursuit of the large cat.

Following a painstaking two-hour trek through treacherous terrain, Jim stopped abruptly to listen to a couple of blue Himalayan magpies and a swarm of buzzing flies. He followed the sounds to a clump of small bushes about forty feet from the trail, cautiously peered over the bushes, then sucked in his breath. There, in a small clearing, were the remains of the young victim.

Years of experience tracking man-eaters had conditioned Jim to such sights, but he nevertheless stared in disbelief. The tiger had eaten over half of the body, leaving a portion of the head and most of the torso. One leg was gone, apparently eaten entirely; the other leg lay nearby, completely severed from the rest of the body. The remains were partially covered with leaves, and only a scrap of her bloodstained clothes was left. Knowing that this particular tiger had a reputation of never returning to a kill, Jim gingerly wrapped the girl's remains in a cloth and returned to Kot Kindri.

Since the tiger was in the vicinity, Jim purchased three buffalo from the villagers to use as bait. Careful selection of sites at which to place the buffalo was critical. Jim found three locations where the tiger's pug marks were prominently displayed, and ordered Mothi to tie each buffalo securely with three pieces of stout hemp rope. Jim hoped the rope would be strong enough to prevent the tiger from removing the buffalo from the immediate area.

As the brassy Indian sun set, Jim and Mothi returned to the village for a much needed night's rest. Around midnight, Jim listened intently to a tiger calling in the distance. Although he had been familiar with the sound for more than thirty-five years, it still filled him with awe. A tiger's roar is very intimidating, especially when heard in the wild.

Two years earlier, Jim had heard about a man-eating tigress near Lohali Village. Reportedly, a young village boy was gathering dry sticks near the edge of the forest when a tigress attacked and dragged him into some thick bushes. His brother, who was nearby, ran back to the village to muster some men and weapons.

When the men, armed with a rifle, returned to the scene, they heard the tigress growling in the bushes. They fired a shot into the air. The tigress charged the men, roaring ferociously, and they beat a hasty retreat. When asked why they had not fired the weapon into the bushes, they replied, "We did not want to enrage it!" Such was the intimidation these fearsome man-eaters held over their subjects.

Dawn arrived with the glorious sounds of the forest's fauna. Birds splashed with vibrant colors welcomed the new day. A troop of langur monkeys was grooming each other and vying for the abundant fruit hanging on tree branches. The sun was quickly dispelling the night's chill. Jim ate a scratch breakfast and quickly departed to inspect the buffalo.

The first two locations revealed no sign of a tiger's visit. However, at the third site Jim detected the pug marks. After following the spoor near this site, Jim was able to deduce that the tiger was not interested in the buffalo. The prints followed the trail to within twenty feet of the buffalo, then veered off into the forest. Although disappointed that the tiger had failed to kill one of the buffalo, Jim was still hopeful.

On his return to the village, the path went down into a ravine containing a small stream, then proceeded up an embankment. When he crossed the stream, Jim came to a halt and stared at some bushes on top of a rocky cliff along the left side of the path.

Jim cautiously approached the stream, then stood motionless for approximately five minutes, carefully scanning the top of the cliff for any sign of the tiger's presence. Nothing stirred. Jim noted the absence of any alarm calls by the forest's other residents. Still, he knew he was in mortal danger. His sixth sense told him that something was on top of the cliff.

Jim surveyed the area to determine if he could maneuver around the cliff. The steep incline on his left followed the stream for a long distance, a route no better than the path. On the right side, there were large boulders surrounded by an impenetrable thicket of bamboo and thorny underbrush. He was trapped, and whatever was on top of the cliff knew it.

Jim raised his rifle to his shoulder and sidestepped crab-fashion along the far right side of the path, keeping a constant vigil on the crest of the cliff. It took several minutes to reach a safe location beyond the cliff, during which time Jim detected no movement whatsoever.

A gradual incline led up to the cliff at that point, so Jim decided to investigate. Cautiously, he climbed his way to the top. When he reached the bushes at the crest, he noticed a large patch of tall grass next to the bushes that was matted down. Some blades were just returning to their upright position. Farther away from the bushes was an area of soft earth that prominently displayed the pug marks of the man-eater!

Jim heard a spotted chital deer some distance away call out an alarm in the same direction the tiger was headed when it had departed the area. Jim sighed and thanked his sixth sense for saving his skin again.

Jim was amazed at how easily a large tiger could conceal itself in its natural environment. During the fifteen minutes he had stared at the bushes, not once did he detect any movement or presence of the tiger. Yet there was abundant evidence that the man-eater had been lying in ambush behind the bushes during the entire ordeal. When its plan was foiled, it had moved off undetected into the forest.

**17**

M aggie knocked on Beth's front door. She was carrying an old wicker basket filled with hot oat-straw biscuits and a kettle of black tea. She had tied her shoulder-length mousy-brown tresses back behind her head, and her beige-laced dress was stained with soil from working in the garden that morning. She heard Beth tiptoe to the door, and quickly tried to improve her disheveled appearance by smoothing the wrinkles from her dress, unaware that her forehead was smudged with a mix of dirt and perspiration.

The door opened slowly—just a crack, but enough to allow Beth a quick inspection of her caller.

"Maggie!" Beth exclaimed. "Oh, please come in."

She opened the door wide, and Maggie saw that she was dressed in formal mourning attire. *Black seems such an unnatural color for Beth, a direct contrast to her cheery disposition*, she thought.

"I've brought you some tea and biscuits," Maggie said as she entered the room. She glanced around and noticed several opened trunks filled with clothes. She turned to Beth.

"Are you going on a trip?"

Beth looked at Maggie forlornly. "No. I'm leaving India—for good."

Maggie couldn't believe what she was hearing and stared at Beth, astonished.

"But *why?*"

Beth turned and sighed deeply. She collapsed into a nearby rocking chair and began to sob. Maggie gently set her basket down and knelt at Beth's side, clutching her trembling hands in her own.

"Jim will be so disappointed if he finds you gone when he returns," she said, concerned. "You know how much he cares for you."

"I know," Beth said, looking off and composing herself. "That's why I have to leave. If I stay, I'll worry myself sick about his safety. I can't just sit here and wait while he's off hunting tigers I've already lost one person I loved to those beasts. I couldn't stand to lose another—I'd go mad."

"Your staying or going won't make much difference in that," Maggie said. "God knows I worry to death when he's out on these hunts. But leaving won't stop him. He has to *want* to stay, and you more than anyone might be able to talk some sense into him."

"He wouldn't stop for me or anyone else, Maggie. He and Kyle are cut from the same cloth—too stubborn to admit the madness of this, and too sympathetic to the villagers to think of their own safety. I'm sorry, but my mind is made up."

Maggie gazed despondently at the floor and nodded her head. "Where will you go? England?"

"Yes, London," Beth said absently, and began to close one of her trunks. "I'll be staying with my Uncle Cecil and Aunt Bea. They have a quiet estate outside of the city where I can rest and calm my nerves."

Beth handed Maggie a slip of paper containing the address. "Please give this to Jim. Perhaps my absence will inspire him to join me and retire from this madness."

Beth looked out the window and smiled sadly, then turned to Maggie. "He won't come, will he?"

"No," Maggie shook her head thoughtfully, "he won't come."

Beth placed her hands on Maggie's. "If he won't come, at least you and Mary should consider it—I don't want to be an alarmist, but you must think of your own safety!"

"What do you mean?"

"Well, I've heard on the latest wire that Gandhi has been gaining tremendous support throughout the country," Beth said.

"Yes, I've heard that too. But you know how these things are, they flare up and then subside. The Indian people realize how much better off they are under British rule. Besides, Gandhi supports a peaceful revolution. He couldn't possibly win without an army or weaponry."

"Perhaps," Beth said, unconvinced, "but still, I don't think you can discount him altogether. He has been quite successful in his boycotts against British products and his workers' strikes. His followers seem to revere him as some sort of god."

"I think you're giving him too much credit, Beth. He has no militia, and we have the best. That's really all there is to it, don't you agree?"

⟨⟩⟨⟩

Jim was depressed. Two more days had lapsed without any sign of the man-eater. The buffalo baits were undisturbed, and no new pug marks had been detected. Jim surmised that the tiger had traveled to another area, and he could do nothing but wait for more news of its whereabouts. During the interim, he provided protection for the villagers when they needed to go to market or work in the fields. For this they were very grateful—Jim's presence provided them with a feeling of security.

Shortly after noon, a *cooee* report indicated a woman had been attacked by a tiger near Chalti Village, four miles west of Kot Kindri. Jim and his men once again gathered their supplies and set off. When they arrived at Chalti in midafternoon, they were immediately escorted to the center of the village where a group of villagers had assembled. There, in the center of the chattering, excited throng, lay the man-eater's latest victim.

How she was still alive was a mystery to Jim. Her head and shoulders were covered with blood trickling from the wounds left by the tiger. The man-eater had missed its mark, the throat, and instead sunk its fangs into her left shoulder. Deep gashes ran from her forehead to the nape of her neck, caused by the tiger's claws as it attempted to grab her and secure a better hold. The petrified woman was breathing roughly, and her eyes were wide open in fright.

To Jim's astonishment, two village men were suggesting that since the woman was sure to die, Jim use her as bait to attract the tiger. Upon hearing this abomination and while watching the woman's look of horror, Jim became enraged!

"No! Get back! Leave her be!" he shouted, pushing the villagers back from the mauled woman. He then ordered the village women to carry the victim into a nearby hut, where she could be attended to away from the curious onlookers. Inside the hut, Jim took from a pack some antiseptic lotion and bandages and instructed the women to tend to the poor victim's injuries. Then he went outside to determine the specifics of the attack.

The village men, who were now ashamed of their suggestion, were eager to assist Jim in ridding their area of this terror. According to their reports, the woman had been returning to the village from a stream seventy yards away with a large jar of water. The tiger attacked her as she stopped to adjust the heavy load. Some of the village men were close-by, and their shouting had caused the tiger to release its hold on the woman and retreat deeper into the forest.

Jim told Mothi to set up camp in the village and, grabbing his rifle and ammunition, walked briskly to the attack scene. Upon entering the forest, he was quick to notice the splashes of dried blood along the trail where the attack had taken place. He proceeded to the stream and detected the tiger's pug marks thirty yards upstream from where the trail crossed.

He went back to the village, purchased two goats, and returned to the stream with the goats and three of his men. After selecting two locations along the stream where he had found pug marks, he instructed his men to tie the goats to stakes.

It was nearing dusk, so they hurriedly returned to the village for dinner and sleep.

Jim heard no calls from the tiger throughout the night. In the morning, following a quick breakfast of tea and biscuits, Jim checked on the goats. He found them both standing next to the straw, grazing peacefully. A cautious and careful inspection of the ground nearby revealed no new pug marks. Jim returned to the village discouraged.

Four more days went by with no results. Jim was impatient and depressed. He had tried everything he knew to attract the man-eater to the goats or to him. On the preceding day, he had draped himself with a village woman's sari and pretended to cut grass and leaves near the edge of the forest. He kept his rifle close at hand, and placed Mothi on a nearby knoll to alert him if the tiger approached. No luck! Jim hated to place himself at the tiger's mercy, but nothing else was working. It was much easier on the nerves to sit up over a kill or track the cat following a kill.

Tracking a tiger would be considerably more difficult if the hunter were unaware of how to use wind currents. A tiger, like other predators, attacks its prey upwind or lies in wait downwind in order to mask its scent. It assumes its human prey has the same sense of smell as other animals; therefore, the tiger will always try to remain downwind to avoid detection.

Knowing this, Jim did not worry about an attack coming from the upwind direction when he was tracking a tiger or leopard. However, if he was moving upwind, experience had taught him to tack back and forth, keeping the likely direction of attack to his side rather than from behind him.

Jim's nerves were stretched to the limit, so he had no choice but to leave Chalti and return to Sem Village, where he could catch a train and get back to Naini Tal for a rest. He reluctantly said farewell to the villagers, promising them he would try to return in two weeks and resume his pursuit of the man-eater. He felt guilty about abandoning them to the tiger's tyranny, so totally empathetic was he to their predicament. As he walked away, he turned to wave good-bye and felt even more remorseful as he noticed the look of utter despair in the villagers' eyes.

Maggie met Jim at the train station in Haldwani. When his gear was loaded onto the buckboard, Jim and Mothi climbed up onto the seat. Maggie flicked the reins, and they began their trip home.

"Mother knows you're after the man-eater. I couldn't keep it from her."

"Is she upset?"

"What do you think?"

"I'll have a talk with her. And how is Beth holding up? Have you seen her lately?"

Maggie stared at the crest of the oncoming hill. She didn't want to look at Jim, to see the hurt in his eyes when she gave him the news.

"She left for England."

"She what? When?" he said, gripping her arm.

"Two weeks ago. She'll be staying with her uncle and aunt outside London."

"Just to visit?"

"She said it would be permanent."

"Why? I don't understand. I thought she was happy in Naini Tal."

"She was afraid you'd end up like Kyle. I guess she just couldn't cope."

Jim stared at the road ahead in silence.

"She does care for you, Jim. And she hopes you care enough for her to leave India and join her in England." Maggie glanced over to see his reaction.

Jim remained silent the rest of the way home. When they pulled up to the house, some of Jim's neighbors ran up to greet him and inquire about his hunt. Jim tried his best to be courteous, but he couldn't get his mind off Beth.

The next morning, Jim didn't have the stomach to eat. Picking over his plate, he asked Maggie, "What do you think London's like?"

Maggie wasn't sure how to answer. She knew Beth had a strong hold on Jim, and he was considering leaving. She also knew, however, that Jim could never adapt to such a civilized world. He had spent his whole life in an untamed land where tooth and claw prevailed. His wardrobe consisted of hunting clothes and a sweat-stained safari hat—not top hat and tails. He thrived on being in the forest in communion with the animals—it was in his very blood. Maggie wanted Jim to be happy, and she knew he would never find happiness in London.

"From what I've read, very civilized. Lots of people, modern conveniences—nothing like Naini Tal."

"I really want to see Beth again." Jim drank his tea, then rose from his chair and walked to his bedroom. Maggie watched him go without saying a word.

Mary rushed into the kitchen, grabbed a cup of tea and a biscuit, and began eating.

"I'm going to be late for market again," she said hurriedly, then noticed the sadness in Maggie's eyes. "What's wrong, love?"

"Jim is depressed over Beth's leaving."

"Beth?"

Maggie nodded. "He's in his bedroom."

"Oh, dear!" Mary walked over to Jim's bedroom, peered through the open door, and saw Jim sitting on the edge of the bed, staring at the floor.

"Jim? Do you want to talk, Son?" she said softly.

Jim looked up to see Mary standing at the door. "Oh, Mum," he said, exasperated, "I don't know what I should do."

"You are very fond of Beth?"

"Yes. She's one of the few people with whom I've ever felt a connection. And now that she's gone . . . I don't know, I'm so confused."

Mary walked over to Jim and softly placed her hand on his shoulder. "You don't have to make any decisions right now, you know. Give it some time. You'll know what to do."

Jim looked up into his mother's eyes. "Do you think I should follow Beth to London?"

"It's not for me to say. The decision is yours, and yours alone. I just want your happiness, dear," she said, stroking his hair. "I think Maggie and I will be able to manage without you for a while." Mary looked into Jim's eyes to gauge his reaction to her comment. All she saw was despair. She really didn't want Jim to go. She depended on him for support—not just financial, but emotional as well.

Jim patted her hand.

"There are so many reasons I want to stay in Naini Tal, and only one reason to go to London," he said.

"Well," Mary relented, "you could always go to London for a visit—test the water, so to speak. If it doesn't work out, you can always come back."

Jim pondered her suggestion. "Yes, I suppose I could, Mum."

She patted Jim on the shoulder, then headed for the door. "I need to get to market before everything is picked over," she said, then added: "I'll tell you this—I'd much rather see you go to London than return to Sem." And then she walked out.

*Sem!* Jim thought, and suddenly his mind was filled with the terrible images of the victimized people. *Those poor souls,* he thought. *I must finish my business with the man-eater.* And Beth's image slowly faded from his mind.

On 5 November, when Jim was at district headquarters, Wyndham informed him that four more villagers in the Ladhya Valley vicinity had fallen victim to the man-eater while Jim was back in Naini Tal. Jim could only shake his head in frustration.

"Damn!" he muttered. "I need to get there straight away."

Two days later, Jim and Mothi were back in Sem. The villagers were surprised and elated to see them. They believed that Jim was like the other hunters who, following weeks of frustration, relinquished the quest and returned home for good. But Jim, feeling fit after his rest, was eager to match wits with the man-eater again. Since the latest attack had taken place three days earlier at Sem Village, Jim decided to wait there until new information arrived on the man-eater.

He was busy cleaning his rifles and checking his gear when a *cooee* message was passed from an adjoining village informing Jim about the presence of a large tiger near Kot Kindri. Anxious to continue the pursuit, he yelled, "Mothi! Assemble the men and load the equipment. Let's hurry to Kot Kindri!" Since this was only a sighting and not an attack, Jim exercised more caution on his journey than he normally would have. The trail to Kot Kindri was entirely through thick forest with deep ravines and rocky cliffs. This was tiger country at its best, affording the cat excellent concealment.

The villagers at Kot Kindri were overjoyed to see Jim and his entourage. The tiger had been seen at the edge of the forest on the north side of the village by several women who were tending livestock. It had growled menacingly at them several times while pacing back and forth along the forest's edge, forcing the women to retreat into their huts. For the next two hours, the tiger had roared in frustration over this lost opportunity for a meal.

First things first, Jim figured, grabbing his rifle and going to investigate the area. The pug marks were definitely those of the man-eater, and Jim was again hopeful he would encounter it. He ran back to the village, requested and received a buffalo and goat from the villagers, and returned to the forest. He had his men tie the animals at locations where the pug marks were prevalent; then Jim selected a large oak tree near the buffalo for his *machan*.

Near dusk, when he was comfortably settled in his *machan,* Jim instructed his men to return to the village. He listened intently to the sounds of the forest while watching the massive, red India sun set beyond the foothills. Enthralled by the beauty of the sunset and the birds, monkeys, and deer calling in their finest melodies, Jim momentarily forgot the seriousness of his mission. Around midnight, exhausted from the journey to Kot Kindri, he dozed off.

D usk and no moon. Jim had been tracking the man-eater for three weeks now and was following the drag marks of its latest kill, a buffalo, through dense forest. He was cautiously maneuvering through thick bamboo and brushy undergrowth when he realized it was becoming difficult to track due to oncoming darkness. He made camp near a stream and, with the wind to his back, kept a watchful vigil for the tiger. It had been a long, hard day, so he decided to take frequent, short naps with his rifle cradled in his arms while waiting for daybreak. His head nodded several times before sleep overtook him.

Suddenly, Jim awoke. The forest was quiet, like a tomb. He listened intently, but the only sound came from his breathing. Frantically, Jim realized the wind had shifted while he was asleep and he was now facing into the wind! He swung around just in time to see the tiger crouched behind him, prepared for its attack. The launch came before Jim could aim his rifle, and he felt the tiger's massive weight crush against his body. Jim heard the tiger's roar just as its five-inch fangs sank deep into his throat. Jim could smell the stench of the man-eater's fetid breath as it pinned him down, strangling the life out of his body.

Jim awoke with a gasp, pushing against a large branch as hard as he could. "Good God!" he cried out, realizing it was a nightmare. He had had this same dream on several occasions over the previous two years, and each time it became more vivid. He was drenched with perspiration, even though the night air was cold. As he slowly regained his composure and his breath, he thanked heaven that he was still alive.

*Such was not the case with that poor young woman last year in Powalgarh Village,* thought Jim. She had been cutting grass in a field next to her village with several other women when a man-eating tigress charged them from a nearby thicket. In the ensuing confusion, the tigress retreated to the thicket and an elderly woman fell off a cliff nearby. When order resumed, the women peered over the edge of the cliff and saw their friend lying on a narrow ledge approximately ten feet down. The old woman had broken her leg in the fall and could not move. A young girl volunteered to stay with her while the others ran for help.

While the other women were returning to the village, the girl noticed that a ledge ran along the side of the rocky cliff. Thirty yards to the right, the ledge was close enough so that she could step down onto it and make her way to the old woman. This she did. After helping the woman into a more comfortable position, the girl crouched down with her knees up against her chest and began conversing with the woman while waiting for assistance to arrive.

Suddenly, the old woman looked up and gasped. The girl turned to see what had alarmed her. Horrified, the girl saw the tigress slowly creeping toward them along the ledge, its glowing amber eyes fixed on its next meal. Escape cut off from every direction, the girl had but two choices—jump off the cliff to a certain death, or face the tiger and possibly save the old woman's life.

When the men arrived from the village, they knew immediately what had happened when they saw the pool of blood on the ledge and the old woman in a swoon. They also knew that the girl had faced every villager's worst nightmare.

Morning arrived without incident, and Jim was greeted by warm tea and biscuits his men had brought. The following night, Jim decided to remain in the village. Throughout the night, he heard the tiger calling off in the distance. The next morning, while checking on the goat and buffalo, Jim noticed fresh pug marks near the goat. However, the tiger had decided against savaging the animal, merely circling it before going on its way up the valley. Jim elected to move the bait animals to new locations and try again.

Two more days and nights went by without any signs of the man-eater. Finally, on the morning of the sixth day, when Jim went to check on the animals, he cried out, "Bully!" Where the goat had been tied was a pool of blood, the severed rope, and pug marks of the man-eater. "Let's go!" Jim took the three men who had accompanied him that morning, and off they went in pursuit of the tiger.

The drag and pug marks were easy to follow until the tiger veered off into a large thicket of bamboo. Jim cautiously circled the thicket, looking for signs that the tiger had exited the area. On the opposite side of the thicket from where he'd begun, Jim noticed the tiger's pug marks. Since there were no drag marks, Jim deduced that the tiger had either left its kill in the thicket after feeding on it or else had repositioned its hold on the goat so it would not drag along the ground. After determining that the tiger had departed the area, Jim and his men began searching the bamboo thicket for the goat.

"Over here, Sahib!" One of the men found splashes of blood and splinters of bone where the tiger had fed on a portion of the goat, but apparently it had departed with the carcass. Quickly, Jim returned to the pug marks and resumed his pursuit.

The trail went over the crest of a hill, then down into a long valley containing a stream. The tiger had followed the stream for four hundred yards, then made its way up a rocky cliff containing large boulders. Along the way, Jim noticed a few drops of blood, which gave him renewed hope that the tiger was still carrying the goat. Tracking through the rocks was especially dangerous as the tiger could be hiding almost anywhere. During the tracking, Jim kept getting an uneasy feeling that they were being followed. However, with the pug marks prominently displayed to their front, he chalked the feeling up to over-taut nerves.

A lavender-hued dusk was now settling on the forest, so Jim reluctantly decided to return to the village and try again in the morning. On their way back, he stopped briefly along the stream to get a drink. When he bent down, he gasped. Superimposed on a footprint he had made earlier was the pug mark of the man-eater. The tiger was stalking them! The track was so fresh that water was still seeping into the imprint. Somehow the tiger had maneuvered its way around them, and the hunter had become the hunted. Jim whispered to his men, "Stay close together, and watch for the tiger. It's somewhere nearby!" The frightened group scanned the immediate area, then carefully made their way back to the village.

Throughout that night, the tiger kept Jim and the villagers awake by pacing along the edge of the forest and bellowing its roar, making everyone uneasy. In the morning, it was gone. Jim had no recourse but to tie up another goat and resume the waiting game.

More days and nights passed without any sign of the tiger. For all Jim knew, it could be miles from Kot Kindri. After a long lunch, Jim provided security for the villagers as they made their trip to market. Later he stood guard while they worked in the fields.

The man-eater was controlling Jim. His every thought and action was haunted by the big cat. He was getting edgy and frustrated. He was not concerned about his reputation, but rather the devastating effect the man-eater was having on the local inhabitants. He had until 24 November to bag the demon; thereafter he was required back in Naini Tal, and it would be months before he would get another chance to return. He could only imagine the additional toll of human lives the tiger would take if he was not successful.

Around midmorning the following day, three villagers from Chalti came running into Kot Kindri out of breath. "Sahib! Come quick! The tiger killed our friend early this morning!" Jim and his men quickly broke camp, packed their belongings, and set off once again for Chalti. During the journey, Jim inquired about the attack. Reportedly, the victim had been watching his cattle graze near the village when the tiger leaped on him from behind. His son, standing not more than ten feet away, saw the attack and watched helplessly as the man-eater dragged his father into the forest.

The man's son led Jim and his men to the location of the attack, then Jim sent him back to the village. Jim, Mothi, and two porters again began their pursuit. The terrain around Chalti was similar to Kot Kindri, so the going was slow and treacherous. Judging from the drag marks, the tiger had its victim by the neck. Once again, the tiger dragged its kill along the stream in a ravine for a distance, then climbed a hill toward rockier terrain, where tracking would be more difficult.

As Jim and his companions followed the pug marks along the stream, they encountered a large king cobra sunning itself next to the water. Avoiding the snake would take them a considerable distance out of their way, so Jim picked up a large stone and threw it at the snake. *Thunk!* The impact of the stone landing next to the snake did not have the effect that Jim had hoped. The cobra raised its head four feet off the ground, expanded its hood, and charged the hunters. Jim didn't want to fire his rifle for fear of alerting the tiger, so his men joined him in pelting the snake until a well-thrown stone caught the reptile in the head. As the snake writhed on the ground, Jim grabbed a large rock, cautiously approached the cobra, raised the rock high above his head, and put the deadly serpent out of its misery.

"Big snake!" commented Mothi as he picked up its tail. The highly venomous cobra was the biggest Jim had ever seen. It measured roughly fifteen feet, had a bright reddish throat, and the back progressed from olive green at the head to its jet-black tail with bands of cream-colored chevrons. Like other big-game hunters of his day, Jim was superstitious, and killing the snake was a good omen to him.

The tiger had proceeded along a well-traveled path surrounded by large boulders and high cliffs; it had then left the path and walked toward a cliff with a narrow ledge that wrapped around its pinnacle. Three vultures circled above the cliff as the men approached.

Jim knew intuitively that the vultures were above the kill, and the fact that they were still airborne indicated the tiger was either feeding on the victim or guarding the remains.

"Mothi, remain here with the men. Stay alert and keep your rifle ready in case the tiger doubles back. I'm going up the ledge alone to see what's got the vultures' attention."

"Y-yes, Sahib," Mothi said, his eyes as large as saucers. He wanted desperately to accompany Jim, but he knew they would make too much noise on the ledge and spoil Jim's chance of getting a shot at the man-eater if it was up there. When his men were in position, Jim began ascending the ridge along the ledge.

Slowly and cautiously he made his way up, careful not to alert the tiger. He inched along the ledge to a bend, beyond which he hoped to be able to see the victim, the tiger, or both. Holding his breath and raising his rifle into position, he slowly peeked around the bend. The vultures were still overhead, but he saw no sign of the tiger. He heard a swarm of flies, indicating the victim's remains were nearby. After several minutes of scanning every nook and cranny of the ledge to his immediate front, Jim quietly shuffled his way forward. The victim's body, lying on the far inside portion of the ledge, finally came into view.

Once again, Jim had to catch his breath as he gazed upon this tragedy. In a mass of blood, leaves, dirt, twigs, flies, and mangled flesh were the horrible remains of what was, several hours ago, a father and husband. *There but for the grace of God*, thought Jim, *could be me!*

Suddenly, the clicking sound of two rocks knocking together jerked Jim back to reality. He discerned from the sound that it came from up ahead, beyond the next bend along the ledge. He slowly made his way forward and, rifle ready, peered around the bend, expecting to be face-to-face with the man-eater.

Nothing. Jim remained motionless as he scouted for signs of the tiger's presence. He noticed a large boulder on the ledge ten feet in front of him and slowly walked over to inspect it. Jim saw bloodstains on top of the rock and realized the tiger had been lying up there cleaning itself. When it had stepped down from the rock, the rock tilted, causing the clicking sound Jim had heard. He could only guess why the tiger had decided to move—the heat from the afternoon sun, hearing Jim's footsteps approaching, or the wind wafting Jim's scent. Whatever the reason, the tiger had made its way down the far side of the cliff and back into the forest beyond.

Jim sat for a moment, allowing his heart to move back down from his throat to his chest. He thought about his men waiting for him, then gazed dejectedly at the setting sun. He had only enough daylight remaining to collect the remains of the victim, round up his men, and return to the village. The thought of returning again empty-handed made Jim nauseous. When he stooped to gather the remains, he noticed other bones lying on the ground back in the shadows. Human bones!

"A lair!" Jim murmured, astonished. "This is the tiger's lair." He could not believe he had actually tracked the beast to its lair. He thought for a moment. Since the tiger obviously had brought other victims to this ledge to feed on them, there was an excellent chance the man-eater would return again—that is, of course, if it hadn't been scared off by Jim when he stalked it on the ledge. However, as quiet as Jim had been, it was unlikely the tiger knew he was present.

Jim realized he would have to leave the victim's remains and everything else exactly the way they were. He felt obligated to return the remains to the grieving relatives, but this would probably be his best opportunity to destroy the tiger before he had to return home.

Since the tiger had just eaten its fill, it probably would not kill again for two to three days. If so, Jim reasoned he could set up an ambush somewhere near the entrance to the ridge where he could intercept the tiger as it carried its next victim to its lair. Unfortunately, the plan would not prevent the man-eater from killing another human. But, provided Jim's plan was sound, it would be the last human the man-eater ever killed.

The plan was not without flaws. The tiger had picked its lair carefully, allowing a front and a back exit. Jim hoped the tiger was a creature of habit, and that it would approach the ledge the same way each time.

Also, the plan was contingent on Jim being able to race the man-eater to the ledge once he received word of an attack, and get settled before it arrived. If the tiger arrived before he did, or if it saw him on the path, it would run off elsewhere. Jim's pony was reasonably fast. But was it fast enough to get him to the ridge before the tiger?

Jim quietly made his way down from the ridge and returned to his anxious and curious men. He scanned the immediate area for the best place for an ambush, hoping to find a large tree along the path where he could place a *machan*. However, the terrain was fairly open, with some rocks, boulders, and bushes.

Jim realized that the space between the boulders where his men had been hiding was sufficient room for himself and his pony. Then he noticed a large crack between two boulders. Looking through it, he realized he had a perfect view of the path until it curved around some blackberry bushes approximately fifty feet away.

By aiming his rifle through the crack, he could shoot the tiger just as it rounded the bushes along the path. Additionally, the boulders would provide him and his horse plenty of concealment. Jim liked the plan. All the tiger had to do was kill once more before Jim departed for Naini Tal, and bring its victim back to its lair.

As Jim and his men returned to the village, they heard the tiger roaring from the forest.

*Jim in military uniform. (photo: Oxford University Press)*

*Jim Corbett's dog, Robin, accompanied him on many hunts.*
*(photo: Oxford University Press)*

*Family group photograph taken at Naini Tal around the turn of the century. From left to right: Mary Doyle, unknown, Jim Corbett's mother, Jim, and Maggie. (photo: Constable & Co. Ltd)*

*Jim at age 22. (photo: Constable & Co. Ltd)*

*Corbett's home at Kaladhungi, near Halduwani (photo: Peter Byrne)*

*Rai Bahadur, who sat with Corbett in his* machans *during the Chuka and Thak hunts. (photo: Peter Byrne)*

*Skinning the Chuka man-eater, with brother of the man-eater's last victim in foreground. (photo: Oxford University Press)*

*An old lady of the village of Kot Kindri, near Thak, whose sister was killed and eaten by the man-eater of Thak. She still mourns her sister and refers to the man-eater as the* shaiten, *the devil of Thak. (photo: Peter Byrne)*

*Two Thak villagers in the dense foliage that borders the Thak to Chuka trail. (photo: Peter Byrne)*

*Main street of the prosperous village of Thak, Kumaon Hills, India. (photo: Peter Byrne)*

*The Sarda River in Kumaon, below the villages of Thak and Chuka.*
*(photo: Peter Byrne)*

*The headman of Chuka who supplied Corbett and his men with all their needs during the hunts for the Thak and Chuka man-eaters.*
*(Photo: Peter Byrne)*

*The Ladhya River, with the village of Sem in the distance.*
*(photo: Peter Byrne)*


*A Thak villager stands on the rock where Corbett shot the man-*
*eater and points to where it stood when he fired and killed it.*
*(photo: Peter Byrne)*

*Peter Byrne at Thak Village with the skull of the man-eater of Thak.*
*(photo: Peter Byrne)*

*The Panar man-eater.  (photo: Oxford University Press)*

*Grandson of the last victim of the Talla Des man-eater.*
*(photo: Oxford University Press)*

*The Bachelor of Powalgarh.* *(photo: Oxford University Press)*

*Jim Corbett and the man-eating leopard of Rudraprayag.* *(photo: Oxford University Press)*

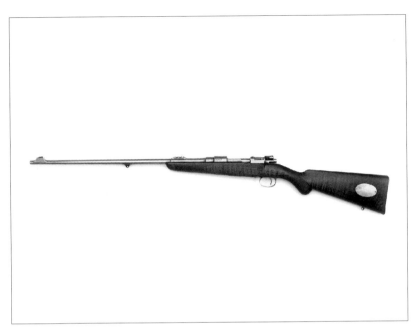

*The rifle used to kill the man-eating leopard of Rudraprayag.*
*(photo: Paul Roberts)*

*Closeup of the presentation plate from the same rifle.*
*(photo: Paul Roberts)*

*Sign in town of Champawat.  (photo: Peter Byrne)*

*A memorial erected to Corbett for killing the man-eater of Kumaon, a rusting tin sign on the road north of the town. (photo: Peter Byrne)*

*(A) shows the position where the man-eating tigress of Champawat probably was when Corbett took his first shot. (B) shows where she was when he took his second shot. The white line shows the route she took after being hit with the second shot ("a narrow ledge that went diagonally up and across the face of the precipitous hill. . ."). (photo: Peter Byrne)*

*Old British bridge over the Champa River north of town. Corbett used this on his route to the kill site. (photo: Peter Byrne)*

*Peter Byrne at the mouth of the gorge in the exact place where Corbett sat when he fired his first and second shot at the Champawat tigress.  (photo: Peter Byrne)*

*The entrance to the gorge.  (photo: Peter Byrne)*

*The Champa River where it narrows just west of the kill site of the man-eating tigress of Champawat. (photo: Peter Byrne)*

*Toward the end of his life Corbett became concerned about the tiger's survival in India. Ironically, after the Indian government conducted an inventory of its wildlife in the late 1960s, it found that most of the remaining fauna resided in hunting areas such as Ranthambhore. Today many of these former hunting areas are national parks. (photo: Safari Press)*

*One reason the habit of man-eating still persists among the tiger is because natural habitat and prey (such as this axis deer) are scarce. (photo: Safari Press)*

*One of the few animals that Corbett disliked was the snake. Fakirs (snake charmers) are common in India, but the danger of their job can be deceiving since most of the cobras have been de-fanged. (photo: Safari Press)*

*Sanitary conditions in India remain poor. Offal from the slaughter houses is dumped at the village perimeters. This tends to attract scavengers and hungry tiger and leopard, increasing the chances of man-beast conflicts. (photo: Safari Press)*

*The daily life of the modern, rural Indian is conducted in much the same manner as it was in Corbett's time. (photo: Safari Press)*

*Signs like these can still be found in modern India, and serve as reminders of the abundant tiger population that once existed. (photo: Safari Press)*

*Maggie in 1963, a year before her death.  (photo: Constable & Co. Ltd)*

*Jim at Dhikala, now a village in the center of the tiger reserve named after him. (photo: Constable & Co. Ltd)*

*Jim with a bag of Tanganyikan lions. (photo: Constable & Co. Ltd)*

*Corbett's grave in Kenya. (photo: Constable & Co. Ltd)*

**19**

D esperation had pierced Jim's normally iron-cast demeanor. Two days had passed without any news of the man-eater. During breakfast of the last day, Jim was frustrated and melancholy. He hated to leave these helpless, gentle people in the grip of continued terror. He had tried everything he knew to outsmart the beast, but it was wise to all his ploys. The tiger had learned well from Jim's predecessors; there was no denying that!

Jim had kept his horse saddled throughout the day, anticipating another attack. But nothing happened. Shortly after noon, he was about ready to give up. His tent was disassembled and folded, and his gear was packed for his return home. The villagers, knowing that Jim was getting ready to go, were quiet and withdrawn.

As he continued with his packing, he heard a shout off in the distance, looked up, and saw a man running toward the village waving his arms frantically. Jim knew it could mean only one thing— the tiger had attacked!

Jim rammed his rifle into the scabbard hanging on his horse, leaped up into the saddle, and spurred the mare into a run. He intercepted the man along the road just outside the village. As Jim reined in his mount, the man stopped and gasped for breath.

"Sahib," he stammered, "the tiger . . . attack . . . kill woman . . ."

"How long ago?" Jim bellowed.

"Not long," the man answered. "Half-hour."

Jim didn't wait for any more information. He spurred his mount into a run again and headed for the ridge. He had played this scene in his mind time and time again. He knew exactly what paths to take to get there in the shortest amount of time. He only hoped he could get there before the man-eater. He *had* to!

Twenty minutes later, Jim was at the ridge. He quickly reined in his horse, jumped down, and looked for fresh pug marks. His heart quickened when he could find none. He had beaten the tiger! He quickly coaxed the mare between the boulders and placed his hand on its muzzle to calm the tired animal. The poor horse was in a lather of sweat from the heat and the fast pace Jim had put it through.

Jim slipped the .450-400 double-barreled rifle from the scabbard and positioned it through the crack. Now it became a waiting game. This was Jim's last hope. He felt confident, even though he realized there were so many things that could go wrong.

Minute after minute went by until Jim realized he had been waiting for a half-hour. Since he didn't know exactly where the attack had taken place, he had no idea how long it would take the tiger to carry its victim to its lair.

Fifteen more minutes elapsed. Jim was becoming discouraged. Perhaps the tiger had taken its victim by the back route to the lair. Maybe the tiger had seen or heard Jim on the ledge three days earlier, and abandoned its lair. Jim could only sigh in disgust and uncertainty.

Convinced that the tiger wasn't coming, Jim decided to creep up the ledge and see if the cat had used the back route. Just as he began to pull his rifle back through the crack, the tiger rounded the dense brush along the path.

Jim gasped. The woman's neck was in the man-eater's jaws, and the rest of her body hung limp, dragging alongside the tiger. The cat was walking at a fast gait, anxious to reach its lair and begin eating its prey.

"This is the last time," Jim whispered as he aimed the sights just below the tiger's eye. Then he squeezed the trigger.

The tiger, stunned and surprised, dropped the victim, jumped four feet into the air, and fell directly on top of a decomposed tree stump next to the bushes. Believing the stump was the cause of its aggravation and pain, the tiger unleashed all of its savage fury on the stump, growling and roaring ferociously as it shredded it to bits with its fangs and claws. Bark and slivers of wood flew about like a barrage of ignited missiles.

Jim tried desperately to shoot again, but only the tiger's hindquarters were visible while it continued ripping at the stump. He cautiously stepped outside the boulders and crept down the path toward the raging beast.

Suddenly, the tiger turned and gazed at Jim. Realizing it was taking its revenge on the wrong object, the tiger bared its teeth and hissed a bloodcurdling sound that signaled an imminent attack. Jim looked into the tiger's fiery eyes of death, glowing, liquid pools of amber that seemed to taunt him. Waves of fear washed across his mind as the beast lunged at him, roaring ferociously.

Jim pulled the other trigger, then watched with great trepidation as the tiger collapsed in a heap at his feet, actually shaking the ground. The man-killer twitched violently and gasped for breath while Jim reloaded the chamber. With one last dying effort, the great cat turned its head to look at Jim, raised its right front paw while extending its claws, and bared its gleaming fangs. Then it quivered uncontrollably, inhaled for the last time, and emitted a low, fading growl. The man-eater's head and paw fell back to the ground, and the animal was motionless.

Jim's knees buckled, and he slowly sank to the ground next to the large carnivore. He ran his hand over the tiger's soft back, estimating it was over ten feet long from nose to tip of tail and weighed more than five hundred pounds!

Jim slowly rose to his feet, then fired his rifle three times in succession to let everyone within hearing distance know that the man-eater was dead. He lit a cigarette and inhaled deeply, allowing the nicotine to soothe his frayed nerves. It was finally over.

A short while later, he heard the joyful clamor from his men and villagers as they approached. The elated men tied the tiger's legs to a thick pole, and all began their journey back to the village. Weeks of strenuous effort in tracking the man-eater had taken its toll on Jim. Nearing exhaustion, his body ached from head to toe.

Despite all his physical ailments, however, he could not help but feel overjoyed in having accomplished the arduous task that had been lain before him. As he gazed in admiration at the beautiful striped cat, Jim recalled a few lines from a poem by nineteenth-century poet William Blake—a poem that described Jim's own fascination with this mysterious animal:

Tiger, tiger burning bright
In the forest of the night
What immortal hand or eye
Could frame thy fearful symmetry?
When the stars threw down their spears
And watered heaven with their tears
Did He smile His work to see?
Did He who made the lamb, make thee?

When the group returned to the village, they placed the tiger on the ground for all to see. Others from adjacent villages traveled to Sem to share in the celebration. Many of the villagers touched the tiger with a hand, then placed their fingers to their forehead, hoping the act would transfer the tiger's courage and power to them.

When the excitement finally abated, Jim inspected the tiger to determine why it had become a man-eater. It was a beautiful specimen, approximately ten years old, and its teeth were in perfect condition. Upon further observation, Jim noticed its right fore-paw was badly infected by porcupine quills that had lodged into the flesh. The wound had festered, causing the animal enough discomfort that it could not catch its normal prey. To survive, the tiger had no choice but to stalk slower prey—which included humans. Jim had seen this often before, and it continued to puzzle him why leopards were smart enough to attack porcupines from the front and avoid getting punctured by quills, but tigers continued to attack this prey from the back.

The following morning, when Jim and Mothi were ready to set out for the train station, Jim was overwhelmed by the villagers expressing their gratitude and wishing him farewell. As he walked to the edge of the village, he turned around to take a last look at a place that was bustling with activity and no longer under the spell of the man-eater's tyranny. Peace and tranquility had returned to Sem and its neighboring villages.

When Jim returned to Naini Tal, he was met at the train station by Mary and Maggie. As soon as his foot was on the platform, the two rushed him, embracing him tightly.

"Oh, Jim, thank Heaven you're well!" Mary exclaimed. "When we got your wire, we were so relieved. Wyndham couldn't be here, so he asked us to let you know that the lieutenant-governor will be arriving today to give you some sort of award."

"I wish they wouldn't bother. Those ceremonies make me so uncomfortable."

"You shouldn't feel that way," Mary said as they walked him back to the coach. "Lord only knows how many more people that tiger would have killed if you hadn't destroyed it."

Jim looked surprised. "I never thought I would hear you say that, Mum."

"Well, it's time I accepted certain realities and learned to live with them," she said as he helped her aboard.

"Well," Jim said with a grin, plopping into a seat, "that's a relief!"

Maggie slapped the reins, urging the horses into a fast walk. "We'd better get home. The ceremony is this afternoon, and the lieutenant-governor does not like to be kept waiting." She slapped the horse lightly with the buggy whip. "Get up, now!"

During World War I, Jim finally found a compelling reason to leave his job in Bengal—to fight for Mother England. He traveled to Calcutta to enlist in the armed forces, but was rejected because of his age. Six months later, England offered him a wartime commission in the rank of captain, to recruit Indians for a labor corps to assist British soldiers in Europe. Jim readily accepted the task, for which he was well-suited. The Indians who knew Jim trusted and respected him, and he had little difficulty organizing a five-thousand-man force.

In 1917, Jim escorted five hundred of his best recruits to France by ship, but the war ended soon after their arrival. While Jim was in France, he wrote a letter to Beth and expressed his desire to see her while he was visiting London en route back to India. In her return letter, Beth welcomed Jim's visit and said she very much looked forward to his arrival.

It was an opportune time to visit Beth. Things were quiet at home, and Mary and Maggie could do without him for a while longer. Jim's mother; Eugene Mary Doyle, his half-sister from Mary's previous marriage; and Maggie were the only three Corbetts still residing in Gurney House, the family home. Jim's older siblings had left home long ago to marry or pursue careers.

Jim was the youngest male in his family—his brother Archibald had died in 1899 at age twenty—so he felt it his duty to care for his mother, Eugene Mary, and Maggie. But Jim's older brother, Tom, was still in Naini Tal and could look after them while Jim was away. So there was really no compelling reason to hurry home.

Jim had always wanted to visit England, and was especially curious to see how much Beth had changed over the years.

As soon as he was settled in his hotel room in London, he
bathed and shaved, then arranged for transportation to Beth's home.
When she opened the door, Jim was mesmerized. She hadn't
changed a bit—still beautiful, still gracious. They sat and caught
up over tea, and then Beth took him on a whirlwind tour of the
city. She was anxious to introduce Jim to her society friends and
to show him how exciting "civilized" life could be.

Despite Jim's eagerness to adapt, however, he found it quite
impossible. He felt awkward with Beth's educated friends: Their
eloquent speech left him tongue-tied, and their political discus-
sions and philosophizing strayed far from the simple survival speech
he was accustomed to. Their interests and his were worlds apart.
London set him on edge too. The hectic pace worked on his
nerves more than any stalking man-eater had. He felt surrounded,
hemmed in by so many people and so many buildings, and everyone was always in a dreadful hurry!

Six days went by, and though their relationship remained
cordial, Jim noticed a definite distance between them. No
matter how they both tried to bridge the gap, it seemed they
were attempting the impossible. Jim knew he was as much of
a bore to Beth's friends as they were to him. He knew Beth
felt differently—she and he had so much in common. But the
more he tried to revive the past, reminisce about their lives in
Naini Tal, the more uncomfortable Beth seemed. Her world
was so different now, and she had trouble connecting with him.
No matter how he felt about Beth, it was clear that they were
on different roads. Hers was lined with theatres and muse-
ums, boutiques and fine restaurants; his was filled with hutted
villages and winding rivers, rowdy pubs and wild beasts. He
still wanted to be with her, but he needed the hunt more. He
thought about asking her to return to Naini Tal with him, but
then realized that she would never be happy there.

One evening, he packed up his gear, kissed her good-bye,
and returned to Naini Tal. It had been a good visit, and though

both were sad at the parting, each knew to what world they belonged, and were content.

One year after his return to India, Jim was promoted to the rank of major and was sent to the Northwest Frontier in India to command the 114th Labor Battalion in the Third Afghan War, known as the Waziristan Campaign. Jim remained in the Northwest territory until 1921 and returned home upon the conclusion of the campaign.

The incidence of man-eaters in the Kumaon Division diminished somewhat over the next eight years. One notable exception was the man-eating leopard that had been terrorizing religious pilgrims traveling through the Rudraprayag region in Garhwal. The government again asked for Jim's help, and he was finally able to destroy the beast in 1926, after it had killed 125 people.

In 1929, Jim dispatched a man-eating tiger in Almora District that was responsible for killing over 150 people. A year later, he destroyed the Chowgarh tiger, which had received notoriety for ending sixty-four human lives. In 1932 and 1933, Jim was asked to destroy man-eating tigers in Mohan and Kanda, which he accomplished without much difficulty. By this time, Jim Corbett's name was famous throughout the whole of India.

A year after the Kanda man-eater mission had been completed, he was summoned once again. This time, a man-eating leopard was the villain.

A serious outbreak of cholera throughout the Kumaon Division had caused a tremendous number of deaths among the Indian people living in the hill regions. In the Nagpur Valley, so many people had died that it became too much of a chore to haul the deceased from the villages, located near the crests of the hills, down to the rivers below, where a proper cremation ceremony could be performed. To expedite matters, grieving relatives simply placed a burning coal in the deceased's mouth and then threw the body over a cliff into the valley below.

Leopards are known to feast on carrion, and one whose territory included the Nagpur Valley satisfied its hunger by feeding on the decaying human bodies tossed down the steep hillside. Eventually, the leopard acquired a taste for this easily accessible new food.

The man-eater problem became noticeable when the cholera epidemic ended in 1927 and the leopard could no longer find dead bodies to satisfy its hunger. Accustomed to its diet of human flesh, the leopard began stalking living humans. At first, the toll of human kills was small. But in 1932 and 1933, the leopard attacked humans with wanton abandon, and by early 1934 its total death toll was approaching two hundred.

Summer months are notoriously hot in India, especially in the central and southern regions. To escape the oppressive heat, many Europeans and Americans vacationed in the northern districts of Naini Tal, Almora, and Garhwal, where the mountainous terrain provided welcome relief. The summer of 1934 was certainly no exception, and that year there seemed to be an overabundance of travelers seeking refuge along the foothills of the Himalayas.

Jim had just arrived at a district conference being held in Naini Tal to discuss matters of concern affecting the district. Normal topics included status of district work-related projects, criminal matters, and visiting dignitaries. Deputy Commissioner Ham Vivian chaired these conferences, held quarterly. The meetings were open to whomever wanted to attend, and Jim made it a point to try to be present at every one.

When he arrived at the deputy commissioner's house, he recognized David Baynes, deputy commissioner of the adjacent district of Almora. This was the first time Baynes had attended one of Naini Tal's district conferences, and Jim was surprised to see him. Baynes was a strange sort of fellow and appeared out of place for a district official. He was in his mid-fifties, tall and robust, and very pompous. It was known throughout the provinces that he had difficulty dealing with the Indian natives in his district, but compromises were made and relationships were improving.

"Hello, Sir David," Jim said enthusiastically as he shook Baynes's hand. "What brings you to our district conference?"

"It's good to see you, Jim. To be quite frank, I've come here to ask your assistance with a rather sticky predicament I'm in."

"How can I help?"

"By finishing a man-eating leopard's reign of terror in my district. I've been having a devil of a time dealing with this one. It's killed nearly 150 people over the past two years, and it has eluded some of the best hunters in India who've taken a crack at it." Baynes sounded desperate and exasperated.

"Are you referring to the man-eating panther in the Nagpur Valley?"

"Precisely."

Jim looked astonished. "When I heard that Morrison went to Almora six months ago, I figured the leopard's days were numbered."

"Morrison is very good, but he gave up last week and returned to Delhi. He did manage to get a shot at the leopard just before he departed, but it's possible that he only wounded the animal. He said he had to return to Delhi to recuperate. Nerves, I guess. The leopard nearly got him on at least two occasions whilst he was in pursuit."

Baynes sighed and continued, "If the beast is wounded, the situation will become even worse until someone finishes the job. The villagers in the area have become outraged that the government has not been able to rid them of this menace, and I'm afraid they might incite a riot if something isn't done soon. I really need your help with this one, Jim."

"I'm sorry about your predicament, Sir David, but I'm overtaxed already with hunting man-eaters in this district. Vivian has been after me to go after the man-eating tiger near Chuka, but I haven't been able to find the time. I've been extremely busy trying to get my coffee plantation under way in Africa. While I'm over there, things pile up back here that have to be attended to. Can't you find someone else who is up to the challenge?"

"I've asked everyone in the provinces I can think of who's good with a rifle. Only a few have accepted the challenge, and the rest expressed reservations about tangling with a man-eating leopard. It's been quite difficult to secure someone."

Jim relished the opportunity to educate someone of Baynes's political stature. Taking a rhetorical stance, he began. "Man-eating leopards are more difficult to hunt than tigers. Leopards never lose their fear of man, even when they turn man-eaters. They continue to hunt their prey during the hours of darkness, making it difficult for a hunter to track and kill them. When the leopard is black, it is called a panther—that is the kind that plagues you now. Its dark color makes hunting it even more difficult than the leopard. On the other hand, man-eating tigers normally lose their fear of man as they continue to stalk humans, and will often hunt during daylight when we are more active and easier targets. Given a choice, I would much prefer to hunt a man-eating tiger than a leopard. Both are risky, but hunting the leopard requires more luck and skill."

Baynes nodded his head. "Oh. Just my bloody luck I'm plagued with a leopard! Well, I figured you would turn me down on this. No hard feelings, ol' boy. I thought I would at least come here and give it a go!"

"Again, I'm sorry I can't help you," Jim said earnestly. "I wish you luck in finding someone soon."

"Thanks. Maybe I'll get lucky and the leopard will relocate into Nepal or one of my adjoining districts—such as Naini Tal." Baynes paused to see Jim's reaction. "Or, hopefully the animal will eventually die from Morrison's shot or from natural causes. I'm keeping my hopes up for any one of these solutions. Anyway, it was nice chatting with you again, Jim. If you decide to change your mind, I'll accommodate you the best I can."

As Jim turned away from Baynes, he stopped dead in his tracks. "Hello, Jim."

It was Jean Ibbotson, wife of the deputy commissioner of Garhwal District. He had become close friends with the Ibbotsons since they had hunted the famed Rudraprayag leopard together. Both Bill and Jean were several years younger than Jim. Bill had worked his way up the government ladder through the successful accomplishment of previous postings. Despite the fact that Bill and Jean were expatriates (born in Great Britain but living outside the British Isles), Jim liked the Ibbotsons. They were honest and compassionate people who took a genuine interest in the welfare of India's poor and underprivileged. Both were avid hunters, and enjoyed Jim's company and knowledge of the forest.

"Jean! What a pleasant surprise."

She was fashionably dressed as always, her clinging, blue cotton dress showing off her figure, and her short, curly bob bouncing about. Jean made up for her plain looks by developing a vivacious and cheerful personality, and was quite a flirt. Her manner captivated most men, and Jim had always gotten a kick out of her girlish manipulations—and played along.

"You naughty man! You've been avoiding me."

"No, I haven't." Jim smiled. "Why do you say that?"

"Woman's intuition," she laughed. "When are we going hunting for pheasant again?" Jean took a long draw on her cigarette.

"When would you and Bill like to go?"

"Tuesday would be splendid—if you can stand to be away from me that long!" She winked at Jim.

*Jean's hot on the trail this time*, Jim thought, and he wondered how far she would really go. He decided to find out.

"Should be fine with me." He smiled and tipped his hat, turning to walk away.

"Whatever pleases you," she said, smiling. "Why don't you stop by at seven in the morning. We're staying at the hostelry."

"Fine. Seven then."

Jean put her hand on Jim's arm affectionately, gave it a small squeeze, and winked. She then turned and walked toward her husband, swaying her body rhythmically as she went, and Jim watched. He could well understand how Jean captivated so many men—she certainly had the gear, not to mention the guts to use it.

Tuesday morning at 7 A.M. sharp, Jim was knocking on the Ibbotsons' door, wearing his khaki hunting outfit and holding his safari hat in his hand. Jean answered the door and invited Jim inside. She excused herself for a moment and walked into the bedroom.

"Are you and Bill ready?" he asked, noticing the quiet inside the house.

"Bill won't be coming," Jean answered from the bedroom. "He had to return to Garhwal yesterday to meet a dignitary. I hope you don't mind."

"No, not at all."

Seconds later, Jean appeared at the doorway wearing her hunting apparel—khaki pants, khaki jacket covering a white blouse, white kerchief tied around her neck, khaki safari hat, and polished brown leather boots.

"All set," she announced as she grabbed her shotgun and cartridges.

It was a beautiful, crisp October morning. Dew sparkled like diamonds on the leaves and grass. A light westerly wind was filling the air with a piney fragrance from the nearby forest. Jim's horse whinnied in anticipation as he mounted, the leather saddle creaking its objection to Jim's weight. In the northeast, the snow-capped Himalayas reached to the crystal blue, cloudless sky.

Jim and Jean rode six miles to a large open field of tall grass. Jim had hunted pheasant here on several occasions, always bagging at least one bird. They dismounted and tied up to a tree bordering the field. They loaded their guns and began walking abreast through the field. They had gone but a few steps when a large pheasant shot into the sky, crying its alarm. Jean swung her shotgun to her shoulder, took aim, and brought the bird fluttering to the ground.

"Nice shot!" Jim said, quite impressed.

"Just lucky," Jean answered, smiling.

Four pheasants later, three of them shot by Jean, Jim suggested they return to Naini Tal. They got back around noon, and Jean offered him lunch. Jim handed the pheasants to an Indian acquaintance and asked that the birds be delivered to his house for cleaning and dressing.

"You know, you're quite good with a gun," Jim said as he sat down in the overstuffed chair in Jean's room with a large glass of brandy.

Jean laughed and plopped down on the bed. "Would you be a dear and help me with my boots?"

"Sure." Jim took another gulp of brandy and walked over to her. He grabbed one boot and slipped it off effortlessly. When he removed the other boot, Jean smiled at him.

"I like you, Jim. We have much in common, you know."

She held her smile, rolled onto her side, and propped her head up with her hand. Jim just stared at her.

"Well, I'd better be off," he said after a moment.

"What's the hurry, love? Can't you stay for a while?" she said in a low voice, and leaned up to him.

Jim stood silently for a minute. It was certainly a tempting offer—but too easy. Besides, he liked Bill too much to risk wounding him so deeply. He smiled, ran his hand along Jean's cheek, and kissed her on the top of her head.

"Thanks for a great day. Now I have to see a man about a *real* man-eater."

"Jim, wait." She stood, clutching a pillow. "I really am quite fond of you." Her expression was sincere. "I don't want you to think. . . . "

Jim nodded. "I like you too, Jean. Give Bill my best, won't you? I'd love to see you both for dinner later this week."

She nodded, her eyes relieved. Jim walked out, closing the door behind him. Jean was touched. Such a passionate man, and yet he reserved it all for the hunt, never for love. It was a quality that attracted her more than his rugged good looks and piercing blue eyes. She felt his essence was a paradox; his casual demeanor and eternal patience with people directly contrasted with his quickness and tense concentration on the hunt. He was an individualist who sought the quiet of the forest, yet devoted his life to helping strangers, and she respected and admired him—and was glad he had left when he did.

A month later, Jim was busy working in his vegetable garden when Deputy Commissioner Ham Vivian strolled up the road leading to the rustic, wooden fence behind Jim's house.

"Hello, Jim!" Ham waved.

"Good day," Jim responded, curious as to the occasion for the visit.

Ham pulled an envelope from his shirt pocket and handed it to Jim. "This letter was delivered to my office this morning, and it's addressed to you. I thought I would deliver it personally. Pretty keen service, right?" Ham chuckled.

"Many thanks, ol' chap," laughed Jim. "You don't have enough to do, so now you're delivering mail?"

"All part of the service. You know how difficult it is to be popular when you're a district official."

"Oh, hell!" exclaimed Jim as he read the letter.

"What is it?"

"It's from the village headman in Nagpur . . . a plea for help."

Jim handed the letter to Ham. The letter was written in broken English, but the intent and desperation were obvious.

———◁●▷———

*A facsimile of this earnest plea to Jim Corbett is reproduced on the following page.*

To Jim Corbett, Naini Tal Village, Naini Tal District
>    June 16, 1934
>    Sir:
>
>    All in the village of Nagpur beseech you to answer
>    our plea for help. We are plagued by a leopard which
>    has killed many of our people for over two years now.
>    We cannot leave our houses to care for our crops or
>    livestock because of this demon that attacks us. We
>    have heard you are a great hunter, with many killed
>    tigers and leopards to your name. We beg you come
>    now and rid us from this problem. Please help us in
>    your mercy and kindness.
>    Your humble servant,
>
>    (signed) Rhatamen Singh

"Gads, he really sounds desperate. What an awful business!"
Ham exclaimed.

Jim continued staring at the letter. "As much as I hate to go,
I can't refuse their request."

"Jim," Ham said, "not one of us would blame you if you did.
You've certainly done your share of destroying man-eaters—and
saved countless lives in the process. You can't run off to help
these people every time they beckon. You're putting your own
life at risk, and at your age, you'd be taking a hell of a chance!"

"Thanks for your confidence, Ham, ol' boy," Jim said with a
grin. "I know that territory as well as anyone in India. If anyone
should go, it should be me. Besides, I just can't sit by and let
those poor people suffer. My conscience wouldn't let me."

"Well, if I can't talk you out of it, the least I can do is wish
you good luck! You're going to need it this time."

"Thanks."

"By the way, if you're interested in talking to Morrison, he's
at the government hospital in Delhi. I hear he's got malaria."

"Good idea," Jim responded, scratching his head. "I'd
like to chat with him before traveling to Nagpur, to find out
what he knows."

Delhi was bustling with activity, as always. Horses, horse-drawn carriages, and motor cars lined the streets, jockeying for openings. Crowds of people moved about like hordes of locusts. Vendors hawked their goods, shouting at the top of their lungs above the noisy din. Dust and dirt were everywhere, on everything. There were dust and dirt in Naini Tal also, but it was expected. Nature intended for it to be there. After all, Naini Tal was in the country. This, however, was city life, and Jim wanted nothing to do with it.

Jim walked up the stone steps to the massive camel-colored hospital in Delhi. He hated hospitals. They symbolized death, disease, and suffering. Jim had been exposed to enough of that in the countryside when tracking man-eaters. But that was nature and survival of the fittest. Here, it was contained in one location, within these walls—walls that contained so much suffering. Jim felt a hollowness in the pit of his stomach as he walked through the entrance.

When Jim entered Morrison's ward, he barely recognized him. It had been two years since he had last seen Morrison, and the man lying on the bed before him with the scraggly face was a pale and thin vestige of what had been a strong, virile hunter.

As Morrison looked up and recognized Jim, a smile came to his face. "Hello, Corbett. Come to pay your last respects?" His voice was shallow, and the words came out with great difficulty.

"How are they treating you, Paul? I hear it's malaria."

"Yes, I've had it for years. This time it's getting the better of me. Are you going after the leopard? Is that why you're here?" He coughed hard several times, spitting up phlegm.

"Yes. I received a letter from the village chief requesting my help. Thought I'd see you first, hoping you could give me some advice."

"Don't go."

"What?" said Jim, perplexed.

"Do yourself a favor, old friend, and forget about it. The leopard's a panther . . . black as midnight . . . the devil himself. It nearly got me twice. I was lucky. It's clever, very smart . . .

seems to know all the tricks. It only attacks at night . . . hard to see . . . hard to shoot. I may have wounded it, but it's doubtful." Morrison's eyes glazed over as he described his futile efforts, and he appeared to be in a trance.

After listening to Morrison's rambling for several minutes, Jim interrupted, "What methods did you try? Were any successful in attracting the leopard?"

"I tried everything—using goats, buffalo, and cattle as bait. Nothing worked. Even followed drag marks at night by using torches. The only time I got a shot at it was when it came into the village at night looking for its next meal. I slept during the day and stood guard at night waiting for the stinking devil." Morrison sighed deeply. "Eventually, I'd hear an agonizing scream from somewhere in the village and run to investigate. By the time I got there, the leopard had vanished with its kill. I couldn't get any of my men to assist me at night. They were frightened out of their wits. The night before I departed, I was able to get a shot off as the cat ran from the village with a small girl. I don't think I hit it. There were no bloodstains on the ground when I looked the next morning."

Jim pondered Morrison's words for a moment. "How was the leopard so successful in getting into the huts at night?"

"Bloody persistence! We used sticks, thornbushes, anything we could think of to keep the damn thing out, but it always found a chink in our armor. I'm telling you, Jim, the animal is the toughest I've ever encountered. Never seen anything like it."

"You don't have to try to frighten me, Paul," Jim exclaimed. "I've already heard many stories about the leopard from others."

"Sorry, . . . don't mean to. It's just that . . . anyway, I wish you luck!"

Jim wished Morrison a speedy recovery and was deep into his thoughts as he walked out of the hospital. *I'll give it two months,* he thought, *only two months. If I don't get the man-eater by September, I'm calling it quits!*

As soon as Jim returned to Naini Tal, he went to his bedroom to begin packing for Nagpur. Robin was on the bed, waiting.

The spaniel had just awakened from his nap, and yawned while stretching out his front paws. He was predominantly liver-colored with several white blotches interspersed over his body. Numerous brown freckles accentuated his white muzzle and paws. Folds of loose skin on his lower jaw wrinkled whenever he was in a playful mood—which was most of the time.

Jim scratched Robin behind his ears, and he licked Jim's hand affectionately. When Jim pulled his hand away, Robin pawed at him playfully, wanting more. He then looked up at Jim with his droopy brown eyes and chuffed through his nostrils. He nuzzled Jim's hand and then immediately rolled onto his back, as he did so often when he wanted his tummy rubbed.

"I can't play now, old fellow," Jim said as he threw some clothes into a canvas bag. Robin whined, rolled upright, then laid his head down on his front paws, watching Jim's every movement.

While hunting the Ladhya man-eater, Jim realized the necessity of having a good hunting dog accompany him. Not only would the dog be able to track the quarry over rough terrain, but he would be pleasant company during those long trips away from home.

Jim had heard about a litter of springer spaniels for sale by an English gentleman who lived in Delhi. When Jim picked the mangy-looking male up from the filthy kennel to inspect him, Robin secured his new home by licking Jim's face. Jim named him "Robin" after the collie he'd had when he was a lad. The collie was not only Jim's best friend but also saved his life from an infuriated Himalayan bear.

Jim had gotten too close to one of the bear's cubs, inciting the sow to charge him. If the collie had not intercepted the bear's charge, Jim would have been mauled. Consequently, the collie took the brunt of the bear's anger and died the following day from the wounds. The loss of the dog saddened Jim deeply, and he vowed that he would never allow himself to become so attached to a dog again.

So, the relationship between Jim and the "new" Robin began in a formal, distant manner. But the dog's playful antics, droopy, sad brown eyes, and long, floppy ears soon overcame Jim's resistance. Although he cautioned himself on several occasions not to become emotionally attached to Robin, it was to no avail.

*After all,* he'd tell himself, *I'm training him to track tigers and leopards, not become a pet.* Robin would often run "point," eagerly following animal scent in areas where Jim would be unable to protect Robin if the dog was attacked. That was his purpose, his function. He was needed to help Jim locate dangerous game and warn him if the large cats were nearby. Jim didn't want to admit it to himself, but Robin was needed to save Jim's life at the expense of his own—just like the former Robin.

Jim had a difficult time training Robin to take hunting seriously. However, Robin's attitude changed abruptly seven months after he'd been adopted when they were out for a walk. The dog chased a peafowl into thick brush. Seconds later, he sprinted out of the brush, tail tucked in, with a young leopard in hot pursuit. Jim didn't have his rifle loaded at the time, so all he could do was yell, "Harrr . . . harrr!" at the cat, hoping the noise would frighten it away.

The leopard continued to shorten the distance between itself and Robin when, for no logical reason, it veered off into the forest. Robin returned to Jim, sat down between his feet, and, with head and ears drooped, whined an apology. That was the day Robin was transformed from a carefree puppy to a cautious, alert hunting dog.

The spaniel had already saved Jim's skin on one previous occasion. They had tracked a large male leopard for four days before Jim could get a shot. The spotted cat moved just as the rifle discharged, resulting in only a flesh wound. Jim and Robin tracked the bloodstains for three hundred yards before diminishing daylight forced them to return to the village.

The next morning, as soon as light permitted, Jim and Robin returned to the area where he had shot the leopard. In a hurry to finish the cat, Jim carelessly began following the blood trail from where they had left off the previous day. He was about to pass a thicket of stunted bamboo trees when he glanced down just in time to see Robin staring at a spot in the thicket. The dog was motionless except for the quivering in his right hind leg—a sure sign of a leopard's presence.

Jim swung his rifle to his shoulder at the same instant the cat charged, and discharged both barrels as the leopard flew past his head. Fortunately, one of the bullets passed through the cat's heart and shattered its spine, killing it instantly.

Nagpur Village was located near the Ladhya River only thirty miles east of Naini Tal. The terrain separating the two villages was hilly and densely forested, but the trails were in good condition despite the rainy season. It was 11 July. Jim had enlisted seven men from Naini Tal to accompany him on this shikar (hunt), most of them familiar with hunting man-eaters. Bhara Singh, one of Jim's bearers, was as eager as always to accompany Jim. When Jim tried to dissuade Bhara from going due to the risk involved, Bhara shrugged his shoulders and replied, "Sahib, I could be bitten by a cobra tomorrow."

When the entourage arrived at Nagpur at midafternoon, they were welcomed enthusiastically by the chief and several other villagers. Jim saw the fear in their eyes as he greeted them. While Jim's men took their gear over to some vacant huts set aside for their use, Jim and the chief walked to the hut where the latest attack had taken place.

As described by the chief, the leopard had entered the hut through a window, grasped a small boy by the throat, and departed through the same window. The attack was so silent that the remaining family members had not awakened and did not realize the boy was missing until morning. Jim carefully analyzed the pug marks in the soft dirt below the window outside the hut where the leopard had jumped down with its prey. The prints revealed the leopard to be a large male, approximately two hundred pounds, in the prime of life. He could not discern if the animal was wounded, but it did not appear to be limping.

As Jim followed the cat's trail to the nearby forest, he asked the chief, "Why didn't the family put thornbushes in their windows?"

"It was very warm that night, Sahib, so they removed some of the branches to allow more fresh air to enter."

Knowing that most animals are creatures of habit, Jim carefully searched the immediate vicinity to determine if the man-eater used the area recurrently to enter the forest from the village. There were no other leopard tracks. He then walked slowly along the forest's edge, hoping to find other points of egress the leopard may have used. His inspection revealed several such places, making it difficult to set up an ambush. *Morrison was right,* he thought, *this one is clever.*

The village was located on a grassy plateau surrounded by densely forested hills and steep cliffs. Streams were abundant throughout the area and within a short walking distance of the village. The area between the village and the forest was cultivated, providing the villagers with needed vegetables.

During the previous three years, the village population had been halved, due primarily to the man-eater. The surrounding hills were populated with small family enclaves, which gave the leopard a variety of places to hunt its prey. This situation provided additional complications for the hunter.

As Jim sized up the situation, the village chief provided an accounting of all the victims over the past several months. Reportedly, the man-eater frequented Nagpur more than the smaller villages, because it offered more inhabitants and a better chance of obtaining a meal.

The people living in these hills were simple folk. Facts that would seem obvious to most others did not to them. Lacking formal education, they learned from experience and what was taught to them from generation to generation. Having had little exposure to the outside world, they became very superstitious and developed a fatalistic attitude. Spirits guided their lives, and they accepted hardship as something that was meant to be and resulted from offending the spirits. Although they anguished over the loss of life like anyone else, the thought of moving away from their village, even while plagued by a man-eater, was not even a consideration. This was the only life and area they had ever known, so any suggestion that they relocate somewhere else while the leopard was at large would fall on deaf ears.

Suffering from the effects of a long, hard day, Jim returned to the village for dinner and a restful night's sleep. That night, Jim had the recurring nightmare—hunting a man-eating tiger in the forest . . . darkness approaching . . . camping next to a stream . . . dozing off momentarily while sitting on the ground with his back to the wind . . . the wind shifting . . . waking up . . . turning around . . . horrified to see the man-eater crouched, ready to pounce . . . the attack . . . the feeling of being crushed by the tiger's massive weight and its fangs sinking deep into his neck . . . the slow suffocation . . . gasping for air . . . dying. Jim awoke, perspiration beading on his face and forehead, breathing hard.

He had long tried to figure out this nightmare, but couldn't. It just didn't make any sense. First of all, he would never be alone in the forest hunting a man-eater at night without Robin accompanying him. Secondly, he would not remain in the forest overnight when a man-eater was at large, unless he was sitting in a *machan* in a tree overlooking a kill or potential kill. The nightmare was so fraught with unlikely circumstances that Jim felt he should be able to dismiss it without further consideration. But for some unknown reason, he could not.

22

Jim spent most of his waking hours trying to educate the local populace on how to prevent the leopard from entering their huts at night. The huts were constructed of poles and mud with thatched roofs. The doorways and windows were merely gaping holes, allowing easy access to almost anything. Jim demonstrated how to intertwine twigs with thornbushes and secure them in the openings at night to permit air circulation and still deter the man-eater. He cautioned them about wandering outside their huts during hours of darkness, and advised them to enter the forest only with at least three other people and to make lots of noise. Also, they were instructed to listen for warning calls from langur monkeys, chital and sambar deer, and peafowl while they were away from their houses. Jim imitated the various calls, and the villagers appeared amused and impressed with his mimicry. Jim provided the same service at the surrounding villages. Additionally, he stood guard while the people sanitized their housing areas and worked in the fields to tend their crops and livestock.

During midmorning on 18 July, three men from a nearby village came running into Nagpur to apprise Jim of an attack. Gasping for breath, they informed him that the leopard had killed and made off with one of their buffalo during the night. Jim grabbed his weapons and, instructing Bhara and two other men to accompany him and the three visitors, set off for the village.

An hour later, they were at the scene of the attack. Jim discerned from the pug marks that the predator was not a leopard but instead a large tigress looking for an easy meal. Upon querying the three men, he learned that the tigress had killed several livestock from this and an adjoining village over the past two months.

Since the tigress was not a man-eater, Jim decided not to destroy it. He needed to teach it a lesson, though, and dissuade it from attacking more livestock. Jim instructed the three men to return to their village, and he and his men followed the drag and pug marks left behind by the tigress and her kill.

The tigress's trail proceeded along a well-established footpath for two hundred yards, then veered off into the forest through a large stand of brush oak. Exiting the scrub oak, the trail went into a deep ravine containing a small stream, then up the far side. Jim and his men had traveled approximately two miles when he heard a swarm of flies and a squawking magpie. He signaled his men to remain still while he investigated with Robin. As he slowly approached a clump of waist-high bushes, he noticed a portion of the buffalo's head protruding out to the one side. He cautiously circled the bushes to ascertain if the tigress was at the kill. Convinced that the cat was not present, he signaled his men to join him.

The tigress had eaten only the rear quarters of the buffalo. Splinters of bone from the hind legs were mixed with blood, leaves, and dirt. Jim was certain the tigress was resting somewhere nearby and would eventually return to the carcass for another meal. He had his men quietly build a hasty *machan* in a nearby ficus tree overlooking the kill, then instructed them to return to the village with Robin and obtain a vacant hut in which they could sleep for the night.

Comfortably settled in the *machan*, Jim listened intently to the forest's sounds. There were no calls of alarm from any animals, so Jim was confident their human activities had not disturbed the sleeping tigress. It was times like this—sitting comfortably in a *machan* watching and listening to the forest's animal inhabitants and observing the colorful flora, that made Jim realize there was no other life for him. He felt alive in this environment, thankful for his many blessings, and wondered if future generations would be able to experience the same wonders of nature.

Three hours passed. Jim had leaned forward in the *machan* to stretch his back when he heard the alarm call of a spotted chital deer. The call came from approximately one hundred yards away to his right front. A ravine was located in that direction. Jim guessed the chital had been grazing in the ravine and, upon seeing the tigress on the move, sounded an alarm. The chital called again from the same direction. Jim searched the edge of the ravine carefully, looking for any signs of the tigress. Moments passed in silence.

Just then, the tigress walked out into the open from a large stand of stunted bamboo trees at the edge of the ravine. Jim was awed by her beauty. "Her majesty" was a deep orange color splashed with vivid jet-black stripes and sported snow-white fur on her throat and chest. She stood quietly for several moments, looking and listening for signs of danger. Convinced it was safe to approach her kill, she quickly trotted over to the buffalo and resumed her meal.

Jim studied the tigress quietly for five minutes, listening to her teeth tear huge hunks of flesh off the buffalo and her powerful jaws crunch effortlessly through bone and sinew. Occasionally, the tigress growled, frustrated over a tasty morsel of flesh that stubbornly refused to release its hold on the carcass.

When the tigress repositioned her body so that she was facing away from Jim, he slowly raised his rifle and aimed carefully. The loud report from the rifle, plus the impact of the heavy slug penetrating the buffalo's carcass five inches from the tigress's nose, had the desired effect. The startled cat jumped approximately three feet straight up, then hit the ground running as fast as she could toward the ravine. Jim had just enough time to send another bullet crashing into a tree as the tigress bounded past it.

He listened to the large cat's flight into the ravine, smashing into anything in its path as it strove to put as much distance as possible between itself and the buffalo. When Jim could no longer hear the tigress, he climbed down from the tree and returned to the village.

In the morning, as Jim and his men enjoyed breakfast at the small village, two couriers from Nagpur came running up the trail.

"Sahib, hurry! The leopard attacked in the village last night."

Jim cursed his luck for not being in Nagpur when the attack occurred and quickly assembled his gear to return there. He instructed Bhara to accompany him and the couriers, and requested his other two men to follow up with the rest of the belongings. They walked at a fast pace, arriving at the village within forty minutes.

Jim was escorted to the scene of the attack by the village chief, who was in an obvious state of panic. Reportedly, the leopard had entered the village around midnight, moving from hut to hut searching for one it could enter without too much difficulty. Finally, out of frustration, it decided to use its claws to tear the thorny branches away from the door opening of a hut containing a family of four. The family members screamed in terror as the leopard savaged the obstruction, growling ferociously. When the man-eater had succeeded in removing the obstacle, it pounced on the nine-year-old daughter and carried her back into the jungle. The rest of the family, terrorized beyond belief, were in a state of shock.

It had rained just prior to the attack, so the pug marks were fresh and easy to follow. Jim and Bhara grabbed the weapons and ammunition, and immediately set off in pursuit of the cat, with Robin taking the lead. They tracked their quarry for a mile through difficult and dense terrain, and finally came upon some bloodstains on the ground. The leopard had repositioned its hold on the girl, causing blood to flow from its initial grip. Jim could only hope the young girl was already dead.

The two men and the dog continued their trek. Jim noticed some of the girl's clothing and hair clinging to a thorny bramble bush as they passed by. They proceeded for two more miles and were approaching a ravine when Jim heard the telltale sound of flies. As they cautiously crept toward the sound, they saw the girl's lifeless body lying near the bottom of the ravine, partially covered with leaves. Jim and Bhara looked in horror at the remaining upper torso. The leopard had eaten everything from the waist down.

Jim finally regained his composure. He realized that the site was ideal for constructing a *machan* in a nearby oak tree and sitting up over the body. So Bhara quickly went to work while Jim stood guard, trying hard to get his mind off the unfortunate victim.

After the finishing touches were made on the *machan,* Jim climbed in and made himself comfortable. Bhara handed him his rifle, the .275 Rigby Mauser, bade him farewell, and headed back to the village with Robin.

As Jim watched the massive red sun set, he fervently hoped the leopard would return to the kill. The moon would be full tonight, and if the sky was clear, he would be able to see the leopard without too much difficulty. Just then, Jim remembered that his only ammunition was the three shells in the clip. Bhara, in a hurry to return to the village before nightfall, forgot to provide him with extra ammunition. *Oh, well,* he thought, *if I can't kill the leopard with three shots, having extra shells won't make one bloody bit of difference.*

Darkness soon blanketed the forest. Now Jim had to depend more on his hearing than sight. He listened carefully to all the sounds of the night, hoping something would tip him off to the leopard's movements. His luck prevailed; the sky was clear and the bright moon tinseled the leaves with shimmering silver.

Around 1 A.M., as Jim's eyelids were beginning to close, he heard the alarm call of a nearby chital deer. His body tensed as he sharpened his senses. Suddenly, his eyes detected movement to the left of the carcass. He gazed at the object intently as he trained his rifle on it. It moved again, closer to the girl's body. It was definitely a large cat, but as Jim was about to pull the trigger, he realized the predator was a tiger. Jim let out a sigh of exasperation. The tiger sniffed at the body, then trotted farther along the ravine.

Moments later, Jim heard another animal crashing through some bushes off to his left, accompanied by loud grunts. Jim recognized the sounds instantly. It was a Himalayan bear—one of the meanest, most cantankerous animals in the forest. The bear approached the body, sniffed at it momentarily, and wandered down the ravine. Himalayan bear and wild boar are the only two animals in the Indian forest that will savage a human. While other large animals will strike ferociously when wounded or angry, they will normally run off after one assault. However, the bear and the boar will relentlessly punish a hapless victim until the unfortunate soul is reduced to a bloody pulp.

Just as Jim was starting to relax again, he was jolted by a boisterous commotion coming from the ravine. He realized from the ferocious growling that the bear and the tiger were having a confrontation. Jim expected the fight to last only a minute, but the two antagonists were waging an all-out battle. The ear-piercing roaring, growling, and thrashing around were making Jim feel very uneasy. Besides, if the commotion did not quickly end, it would dash all hope of seeing the leopard.

Seconds later, the bear came running up the hill with the tiger in hot pursuit. Jim shuddered in fear as he watched the bear head straight for the tree in which he was perched. "Har! Har! Har!" he yelled at the top of his lungs.

It was too late. The bear, desperate to escape from the tiger, leaped at the tree and began ascending. Jim had only a second to react. Swinging the muzzle toward the bear's head, he quickly pulled the trigger. The shot was true, and Jim watched anxiously as the bear released its grip on the tree trunk and fell backward onto the tiger. Startled by the rifle's blast and the falling bear, the tiger ran back down into the ravine as though it had been scalded.

As Jim regained his breath, he thought about his dilemma. He had only two shells remaining and nearly four hours until daylight. So he kept one eye on the prostrated bear at the foot of the tree and his finger on the trigger.

As soon as dawn arrived, Jim fired another round into the bear's skull to ensure it was dead, and descended from the tree.

He carefully wrapped the girl's remains in a cloth, then headed for the village. He was surprised that Bhara and Robin had not met him at the tree with hot tea and biscuits as they normally did. But it was still early in the morning, and he would probably run into them along the trail.

As Jim rounded a bend in the trail approximately halfway to the village, something caught his eye. It was a piece of cloth hanging from a thornbush. Jim knelt to investigate, and saw some dried blood mixed with pug marks on the ground. Jim gasped in horror as he recognized the cloth. It was from a shirt he had given to Bhara the previous month! Closer inspection of the pug marks showed they belonged to the leopard. "Oh, no!" Jim cried aloud. "Please, God, not Bhara!"

Jim searched the surrounding area until he found more pug marks leading away from the vicinity. Adjacent to the cat's paw prints was the telltale line in the dirt from Bhara's foot. Jim cursed his luck again. He had only one cartridge remaining, leaving him with only one recourse. He had to return to the village to obtain more ammunition before he could track the leopard. In a flash, Jim ran to the village.

Ten minutes later, Jim was at the hut explaining to his men and the village chief what he had found. One of his men told Jim that Bhara, realizing he had forgotten to leave Jim extra ammunition, had decided to return to Jim's location. They rationalized that since it was after dark, Bhara would stay with Jim until morning. Jim grabbed several more cartridges, then ran back up the trail with Robin at his heels.

Upon reaching the attack site, Jim and Robin went to work. Jim tracked with great urgency. He kept reminding himself to slow down, but if Bhara was still alive, Jim was not about to waste any time locating him.

For two and a half miles they followed the leopard's trail through thickets, bamboo, streams, and over rocks. As Jim was forcing his way through a dense thicket of undergrowth, he stumbled over an object and fell forward. As he stood up, he noticed blood on his shoe. Puzzled, he turned around to look at the obstacle. It was Bhara!

Mortified, Jim knelt and began brushing the leaves and dirt from Bhara's body. The man's legs and buttocks were missing. Intestines were protruding from his stomach cavity. Jim sat down, anger and frustration filling his heart.

A minute later, Robin walked over to Jim and licked his hand compassionately. As Jim stroked Robin's head, he slowly regained his composure. He was in no mood to sit up over Bhara's body, so he wrapped up the remains and returned to Nagpur.

When Jim shipped Bhara's remains back to Naini Tal, he sent a message to Maggie asking her to comfort Bhara's widow and to take care of any financial requirements the family might have. He would ensure they were in need of nothing; Bhara had gone into the situation knowing Jim's character—everybody who knew Jim knew he took care of his men.

**23**

Throughout the next two weeks, the leopard continued to stay one step ahead of Jim. It continued to attack Nagpur and the surrounding villages at random, leaving Jim exhausted from being constantly on the run and in pursuit. He sat up over several more kills, but the leopard never returned. He tried every tactic he knew to entrap the man-eater, but to no avail.

Everything he had been told about the animal by Morrison and others was true. It never returned to a kill—probably because it had been shot at by a hunter when it returned to a kill some years ago. It never attacked any domestic animal, used as bait or not. It attacked only during the hours of darkness, thereby masking its movements. It chose villages at random and used different points of entry and exit each time, making it difficult for Jim to establish a pattern and set up an ambush.

He was stumped. Unless he could think of something to alter the status quo, the advantage would continue to be in the leopard's favor.

One day, as Jim was cleaning his weapons and contemplating his options, a thought came to mind. The idea would require some work by the villagers, but he believed they would support him. He summoned the Nagpur village chief and approached him with the idea first, hoping that if he agreed, he could convince the rest of the villagers. Besides, if the village chief implemented the suggestion and it was successful, he could take credit for it. As the chief entered Jim's hut, Jim began his art of persuasion:

"I have a plan, but I need your advice. As long as the villagers sleep in their own huts at night, the man-eater has us at a disadvantage. It can enter any hut it wants in this village or those nearby. I cannot guard every hut all the time throughout the night.

"What if we built a hut large enough for everyone in the village to sleep in at night, just until the leopard is destroyed? That way we could post guards throughout the night while the rest of the people sleep. The guards could be two or three men who sit inside the hut by the windows and doorway and alert me if they hear or see the leopard approaching. I would sleep during the day so I could stay awake at night." Jim paused for a few seconds.

"Of course, this same routine would also have to be implemented in the other villages, unless they prefer to travel to Nagpur each evening and sleep there. This would reduce the number of places where the leopard could attack us. I could randomly rotate among the villages, thus improving my chances of being at the right place when it attacks."

The village chief pondered the proposal while rubbing his bearded chin. Realizing that he would be exalted by the villagers if this idea was successful, he concurred. *At least,* he thought, *it may save some of my people from the demon.* While the chief was informing the villagers of his great idea, Jim found a place within the village that would accommodate a hut large enough for everyone, and began marking out the dimensions.

The enthusiasm among the local populace was overwhelming. Seven of the villages elected to sleep in Nagpur; the two others decided to build their own sleeping hut. Jim was ecstatic. Now he had to rotate among only three locations at night, cutting the leopard's advantage significantly.

When lives are at stake, it is amazing how fast a project can be completed. The sleeping quarters were all ready for occupancy by the sixth day. During the construction period, the man-eater took two more lives. At each location, Jim instructed the people about the guard system. The guards at the two locations where Jim was not present were to bang on a pan with a stick when they saw or heard the leopard. It was hoped that this would frighten the man-eater away.

Although the animal continued to strike over the next three weeks, the frequency of its attacks was diminished due to the new strategy. Consequently, the leopard became more aggressive in its attacks, and more clever at removing obstacles wedged in the doors and windows.

At 9:15 A.M. on 5 September, Jim awoke abruptly from sleep upon hearing three gunshots off in the distance. Since Baynes had given his assurance that no other hunters would be allowed in the vicinity during his hunt for the man-eater, Jim was perplexed. He made a mental note about the direction from which the shots appeared to come, ate a scratch breakfast of biscuits and tea, then set off to investigate.

It was daylight, so Jim did not have to worry about the leopard. He had walked at a brisk pace for approximately two miles when he noticed a campsite near a stream to his left. As he approached the site, he noticed a *machan* in a large ficus tree and two goats tied to a stake within thirty yards of the tree. The campfire was still smoldering and upon closer observation, Jim noticed the footprints of two men in the dirt. Thirty yards from the campfire, he found hoofprints from three horses. Apparently, one of them had been used to pack in equipment and provisions. The signs indicated the men had made a hasty departure just before Jim arrived.

Jim and Robin walked in concentric circles around the campsite, searching for other clues. On the second revolution, Jim stopped to look at a large pool of blood on the ground near some bushes. Standing quietly, he carefully surveyed the surrounding area. Suddenly, a deafening roar erupted immediately to Jim's front—right where Robin was!

Robin let out a piercing yelp, which was followed by another roar from his attacker. Jim ran ahead briskly, clicking the rifle's safety catch off. As he broke into a clearing, he saw Robin writhing on the ground, blood covering his right shoulder. Sensing mortal danger, Jim stopped dead in his tracks. Just then, he heard the warning hiss of a tiger. He gazed at a clump of thick bushes about ten feet to Robin's right and saw the tiger crouched, ready to strike. Jim aimed quickly and pulled the trigger. The tiger rolled to its side and stopped breathing. Jim pelted the animal with two stones and, assured that it was dead, ran over to Robin.

The dog was whimpering from his wound but wagged his stubby tail as his master approached. Jim spoke soothingly to calm Robin while removing antiseptic lotion and bandages from his jacket. The damage was serious. Jim bandaged Robin the best he could, and realized he had to take him to a veterinarian right away.

When the dog had been made as comfortable as possible, Jim walked over to the tiger, puzzled why it had not finished Robin off. When he saw the gunshot wounds in the tiger's hindquarters, it made sense. The tiger had been the recipient of the shots Jim had heard earlier in the morning, which eventually crippled it to the point where it could not walk or run. It had merely hid in the bushes and attacked Robin when he got too close.

Jim was furious! Not only were these hunters not supposed to be hunting in this area, but they had wounded a tiger. And because they failed to finish the task, it had attacked Robin. There were no vets in Nagpur, so Jim's only hope of saving Robin was to transport him to the district capital of Almora. As he gingerly picked the dog up, he noticed that the hoofprints of the three horses went off in the same direction he was heading. Astutely, he observed that one of the horses had a small piece chipped out of the shoe on its right rear leg.

"If they're in Almora," Jim muttered angrily, "I'll find them."

He walked the fourteen miles to Almora Village as fast as he could. Occasionally, he spoke comforting words to Robin during the trek, noticing the trusting look in his eyes. As soon as he arrived in the village, he went to Baynes's residence to report the incident. Baynes's servant escorted Jim and Robin to the village veterinarian, and as soon as the dog was in the vet's care, he returned to Baynes's house.

"Did you see two men ride into the village earlier this morning with a packhorse?" Jim's voice quivered with anger.

Baynes sensed his anxiety. "I didn't. But my cook saw them come in. She said they went over to the hostelry. That's where they've been staying the past week or so. How will you be sure it was them?"

"I'll know as soon as I see their horses." Jim grabbed his rifle and walked to the door.

"Do you want any of my security men to accompany you?"

Jim gritted his teeth. "No! If they're the ones, I'll deliver them to you."

When Jim approached the hostelry, he noticed several horses tied to the fence in front. It took him only a minute to identify the horse with the defective shoe. A pack horse was tethered next to it. Jim entered the lobby and saw two men sitting at the bar, talking boisterously. One was about Jim's size, but stockier. He was rough looking with a two-inch scar on his right cheek. The other man was smaller and thinner. Both were wearing safari hunting outfits. Jim deduced they were vacationing in Almora to do some hunting and had decided to poach in the Nagpur vicinity despite the prohibition. Jim placed his rifle next to the door and walked over to the men.

"Either of you two own the black mare out front?"

"Why, do you want to buy it?" questioned the large man snidely.

"I tracked it into the village from a poaching site fourteen miles southeast of here. There were three horses—one was packing gear. I presume you are the two men I'm looking for." Jim stood tense, his feet spread apart.

"You can't prove we were poaching!" proclaimed the wiry man.

"I most certainly can! The tiger you wounded attacked my dog and damn near killed it." Jim was breathing hard. "I had to kill the tiger and carry my dog here to Almora for treatment. Now, how about going with me to the district commissioner's office?"

The two men glanced at each other briefly. Then the larger one lunged at Jim, pushing him to the floor. As he attempted to make a break for the door, Jim grabbed his foot, tripping him. In a second, Jim was on top of the man and pulling him up. The man swung his fist. Jim blocked the punch and landed a blow on the stranger's chin. As the poacher lay writhing on the floor, Jim looked over to the other man to determine his intentions.

"I don't want any part of this! No trouble!" He held his hands up as a sign of surrender.

"You broke my jaw!" cried the large man as he cupped his hand to his mouth.

"If my dog dies, I'll break more than your jaw! Now get up!"

Jim grabbed his rifle and escorted the two men to the commissioner's house. Baynes ordered two policemen to escort the poachers to the district detention center, from where they would be transported to province headquarters for trial later in the month. Jim filled out the necessary paperwork, then went to check on Robin.

"How's my dog?" Jim asked as he entered the vet's office.

The vet looked up as he was taping a large bandage to Robin's leg. "Not bad. I treated the wound the best I could, but he'll need a lot of rest and care."

"I need to return to Nagpur to track the man-eater." Jim stroked Robin's head. "Please look after him until I return—about a fortnight or so. He means the world to me, and I'll certainly compensate you for your trouble."

"Don't worry, Sahib. Your dog will be treated as my guest."

Jim walked to the door, turned to look at Robin lying on a blanket in the opposite corner, then exited the hut en route to Nagpur.

For the next two weeks, the leopard continued its reign of terror over Nagpur and the two other villages where the local inhabitants congregated every evening. Four more villagers were carried away by the man-eater even as Jim made every effort to encounter the beast. It seemed he was always one step behind. When he was spending the night in Nagpur, the leopard would strike in one of the other villages, and vice versa.

Frustrated by his lack of success, Jim had the villagers light torches at night and place them around the sleeping huts to dissuade the leopard from attacking. This, like the other strategies, did not work. The man-eater simply got bolder in its attempts and nearly always managed to find a victim.

Jim did not have to perform the distasteful task of following up on the attacks and having to bring back any grisly remains of the victims to their grieving relatives. But seeing and hearing their anguish following an attack was painful enough. Jim was beginning to feel their pain and suffering. He knew he had to do something fast. He was running out of time, and he did not want to leave these helpless people living in terror.

Finally, on the night of 17 September, the leopard made its first mistake. It attacked the hut where Jim was standing guard. It happened early in the morning, before dawn. Seated inside the doorway, Jim was just nodding off to sleep. As always, the people had secured the doorway and windows with plenty of thorn branches and vines.

Jim had closed his eyelids for just a second when he heard a noise—not loud, just a slight scratching. He listened carefully, trying to filter out the sounds from those of the sleeping villagers. Then a low, guttural growl came from beneath one of the windows. Jim slowly and silently trained his rifle sight on the window opening. There was only a quarter moon, so visibility was limited. Fortunately, everyone else inside the large room was asleep; no one was alarmed.

As Jim stared at the window opening, he saw the leopard's paw pulling at the branches. Several times the massive black paw pulled at the entwined vines, trying to dislodge the only obstacle between the leopard and its next meal. Suddenly, the man-eater grabbed a thick branch with its teeth and, yanking hard, jerked the entangled mass of branches loose from the opening.

*Come on in, Spots,* thought Jim as he released the safety on his rifle and tightened his finger around the trigger. Before Jim could react, however, the leopard leaped through the opening into the hut. Jim shouted to alert the sleeping villagers, but the predator already had grabbed a small girl by the throat with its teeth and was heading back through the window. The leopard's proficiency and quickness astounded Jim. The man-eater was ready to leap onto the ground outside, and Jim aimed his rifle at the window opening.

"Damn!" he yelled as he lowered his weapon. Panicked villagers scurrying about between him and the window hindered his shot. The startled villagers were shouting and yelling and running into each other inside the dark room. When Jim was finally able to restore order, he had three men light torches so he could investigate outside the hut. He removed the branches in the doorway, then cautiously proceeded outside with the torchbearers.

By now dawn was breaking, and, with the aid of the torches, Jim was able to search the ground around the hut. He found some bloodstains from the young girl on the window ledge and on the ground directly beneath the window. As he followed the cat's pug marks toward the forest, he found more blood. Since the dawn's light was becoming more pronounced, he decided to track the leopard, hoping to surprise it as it ate its kill.

Jim grabbed some biscuits and his twelve-bore double-barreled shotgun, then began his pursuit. Each of the shells he took along contained eight slugs, which would give him a better chance of hitting a charging leopard than would a single bullet.

Between the pug marks, drag marks, and occasional bloodstains, tracking the leopard was easy. Jim's only fear was that it might rain and erase the tracks before he located the man-eater. He tracked the great cat relentlessly through forest, over hills, into ravines, over rocky terrain, and across streams for approximately three miles. The follow-up was painstakingly slow due to the rugged terrain and the threat of attack. He wished fervently that Robin was with him. The dog's keen sense of smell would have permitted him to travel much faster through the more difficult areas.

As he rounded a sharp bend in a trail through a treacherous area containing large boulders and dense scrub, he heard the flies. The sound was unmistakable. Shotgun ready, he peered behind a large bush and drew in a breath. It was the girl—or, rather, what remained of her. As with previous kills, the man-eater had consumed the lower portion of her torso, leaving the chest and head. One arm had been bitten off at the elbow.

Jim sighed in frustration. Though he thought the leopard was probably miles away resting from the meal, he decided to sit up over the girl's remains anyway. He had nothing to lose, and there was always the chance, albeit slim, the man-eater would return for another meal. Jim located a large oak tree nearby to sit in, and cleared away any obstacles between the body and the tree that would impede his observation. When Jim was comfortably seated in the tree, he took out his biscuits and ate lunch.

There was no sign of the leopard throughout the afternoon. In fact, the forest was very peaceful. At 5 P.M., Jim climbed down from the tree, wrapped the girl's remains in a cloth, then headed for Nagpur.

A half-hour later, the skies turned black and the wind began to howl. Jim knew what he was in for. It was still the rainy season, and torrential rains were not uncommon at this time of year. Jim found shelter under a rocky ledge as the first drops fell to the earth.

Two hours later, the storm finally subsided. It was one of the worst Jim had ever encountered. The wind blew incessantly while the rain came down in sheets. Although the ledge provided shelter from the lion's share of the storm, the wind-whipped rain managed to soak most of Jim's clothing. When Jim stepped out from under the ledge, he was astounded by the destruction the storm had left in its path. Small trees were leveled, many bushes were uprooted, and large branches were broken off the bigger trees. Only one hour remained until darkness, so Jim hurried on his way back to Nagpur. When he rounded a corner in the trail approximately two miles from the village, he stopped dead in his tracks.

The stream he had crossed earlier in the day was now a raging, muddy torrent. Worse, the log bridge was completely gone, swept away by the swift current. The flash flood made the stream, which was now a river, impossible to cross. Knowing he was stuck here until morning, Jim tried to make the best of a bad situation.

He thought about his predicament. He was soaked to the skin, had no food, and could not build a fire because everything in the forest was saturated. The hunger he could deal with, but having to sit outside overnight while wet and cold did not appeal to him at all. Worst of all, a man-eater was at large, and it used this trail frequently at night.

Jim analyzed his surroundings carefully. His primary consideration was survival; comfort was secondary. The area where the trail intersected the river was fairly open, preventing the leopard from attacking him from a tree limb overhead. He would not have to worry about an attack from the river side. It was flowing too rapidly and was too wide for a leopard to leap across. Therefore, by sitting with his back to the river, Jim had to be concerned only with a ground attack from the front or sides. Also, since the wind was coming from his right front, he knew the leopard would stalk him only from his left side. That was, of course, if the leopard was in the area and elected to attack.

Jim thought about returning to the ledge where he had sought refuge during the storm, but not enough daylight remained. Resigned to his fate, he placed ample leaves on the ground to make his seat more comfortable, then constructed a makeshift backrest out of stout twigs and vines. When it was completed, Jim sat down and tried to make himself as comfortable as he could. The moon would be up in about two hours and might provide enough light to enable him to see anything moving nearby. He had to stay awake until then. If the man-eater was going to attack him, it would most likely do so before the moon rose.

**25**

Jim rocked back and forth in an attempt to fight off sleep. The day had been long and tiring, and exhaustion was catching up to him. The wind had died down almost completely and despite the wet clothes, Jim was beginning to relax.

"I can't let myself fall asleep!" he whispered. He pinched his leg repeatedly, hoping the pain would cause his drowsiness to subside. He checked and rechecked his gun, ensuring the chambers were loaded and the safety was off. Despite all his efforts, his weariness finally won. His head nodded several times, then he fell asleep.

Dusk and no moon. Jim had been tracking the man-eater all day, and was exhausted. He made camp next to a stream. He sat down with his back to the wind and cradled his rifle in his arms. Feeling the strains of the day, he was finally overtaken by sleep. He awoke, startled. He realized the wind had shifted 180 degrees. He turned around and saw the man-eater crouched, ready to pounce. Before Jim could react, the tiger attacked, roaring ferociously. Its fangs sank deep into Jim's throat, strangling the life out of his body. He could feel the tiger's massive weight pinning him down as he gasped for breath.

Jim awoke, his hands clasped around his throat. "God almighty!" he cried, "the nightmare!" As he inhaled deep gulps of air into his lungs, a cold, stark realization hit him:

"God! *This is my nightmare!*" he stammered as he sized up his situation. There were subtle differences, but the similarities were too uncanny—too eerie! Here he was, alone, camped overnight next to a stream . . . spent all day tracking a man-eater . . . sitting with his weapon cradled in his arms . . . exhausted and then overcome by sleep. An unforeseen set of circumstances had placed him in this current dilemma—Robin becoming injured and unable to accompany him . . . the torrential rain flooding the river and washing out the bridge, preventing him from returning to the village.

"But," he rationalized as beads of sweat fused on his forehead, "the man-eater in the dream was a tiger, not a leopard. Or was it?" He tried desperately to recall the specifics of his recurring nightmare. He had always assumed the man-eater to be a tiger. He had never given it much thought . . . until now.

Just then, Jim felt he was in danger—mortal danger. It was a sixth sense he had, on which he always relied. He gazed into the darkness around him, trying hard to detect any movement or noise. He noticed the wind had shifted and was now coming from his back. If the leopard was stalking him, it could come from the front or either side. He sat motionless—listening . . . watching . . . waiting.

Jim wondered about Robin's future if anything happened to him. *Who would take care of him? Would he be all right?* Questions kept popping into his mind for which he had no answers. The wind was beginning to pick up now, making it difficult to hear anything approaching. The moon was just rising above the horizon, but was still hidden behind the trees. Occasionally, Jim would catch a glimmer of moonlight shimmering through the branches. The intermittent illumination gave him cause for hope.

The wind caused the shadows of tree branches to dance on the ground in the moonlight. He studied every shadow carefully, knowing any of them could be the man-eater. Suddenly, his eyes caught a shadow to his front that was not moving, even while the wind was blowing. *Could it be the leopard?* he thought. He gazed at it intently, studying its shape and size. It was fairly round, like a large cat crouched into striking position. The object was approximately thirty feet from him. The harder he looked at it, the

sponse, then said, "It's okay, Jim, I'll tell the governor you can't do it." Bill turned to walk away.

"No, wait," Jim blurted. Bill spun around. "I'll try for one month, and only one month. If I haven't destroyed it by 15 November, I'm returning home."

Maggie winced.

"Fair enough," Bill remarked. "Same conditions as always?"

"Yes."

"Good. I'll notify the governor immediately."

"One other thing, Bill," Jim said as he grabbed Bill's arm.

"What's that."

"This will be the last time. I want your and the governor's promise that there will be no more requests."

"You have mine, and I feel certain the governor will agree to this also." Bill adjourned the meeting and walked toward his house with Jim.

"By the way, Jim, the governor could not get approval on our request to set aside another wildlife sanctuary in the Kumaon Division."

"Why? I thought he was in favor of the idea."

"He was, and still is. However, he can't sell the idea to the viceroy because of the political situation."

"What do you mean?"

"The viceroy is unwilling to make a decision on this issue. Considering the political turmoil in India right now, he's got larger problems to resolve."

"But we've been trying to establish another wildlife reserve for the past four years!" Jim sounded exasperated.

"I know, and I feel the same as you about protecting the tiger and its habitat. You should feel fortunate that Lord Hailey was able to establish the reserve in Garhwal. But let's face it, if India receives independence, it will be up to them to protect their wildlife. They could easily reverse anything we implement. Considering the anti-British sentimentality that's been brewing lately, I expect them to renounce anything we attempt to do."

Jim sighed. "I see your point. I only hope they do something before it's too late. I cannot imagine an India without tigers, leopards, and elephants."

"Nor I," Bill agreed. "But if it's any consolation, we'll probably be dead and gone by then." Jim just shook his head in disgust and headed back to his house.

Jim's success rate at destroying man-eaters made him the prime candidate every time one appeared in the provinces. Although his heart bled for the villagers who were killed by a man-eater, he realized his hunting prowess was no longer what it used to be. He had given up hunting large game for sport in 1930, and devoted his efforts to wildlife preservation and filming animals with his movie camera.

Although physically fit, Jim's sight and hearing had deteriorated over the past several years, and his reflexes were not as sharp. Better than anyone else, Jim knew the critical importance of acute senses when hunting these beasts. Pitted against a predator that was stronger, faster, and stealthier than humans, Jim's only advantages over his opponent were his marksmanship and his vast knowledge of the animals in the forest. Well, he had one other advantage, which most people would discount—his sixth sense.

Jim made it a rule to never hunt man-eaters with another hunter, due to the risk involved. However, he made an exception with Bill Ibbotson, whom he called "Ibby." They had hunted together for a long period in 1926 to destroy the Rudraprayag man-eating leopard. During that hunt, Jim developed a tremendous respect for Ibby's hunting skills and courage. So when Ibby suggested they hunt this man-eater together, Jim was not at all opposed to the idea.

Jim and the Ibbotsons arrived in Sem on 12 September, shortly after hearing about the man-eater's latest victim. Reportedly, a woman had been working in a terraced field near the Sem village when the tigress sprang on her from a bank of tall grass bordering the field. She screamed only once before the man-eater clamped its powerful jaws around her neck, bounded up a twelve foot embankment, crossed an open field, then disappeared into the forest. Her twenty-year-old son was standing not more than ten feet away when the tigress attacked, and he witnessed the tragic event. He was so petrified with fear that he could do nothing to assist his mother.

Two days later, a large party of villagers from Sem gathered enough courage to follow the tigress's trail into the forest. All they found were shredded, bloodstained strips of the woman's clothing and small splinters of bone.

Shortly after Jim got settled in Sem, he surveyed the area to look for any signs of the man-eater. He managed to find fresh pug marks of the tigress in the sand along the Ladhya River near the village. This gave him hope the tigress was still in the area.

He had three buffalo sent to Sem to use as bait. When they arrived, Jim had his men secure the buffalo at locations around Sem where he thought the man-eater would most likely find them. For the next three days, Jim and Ibby inspected the buffalo, hoping the tigress would take one. Although they found fresh pug marks near the buffalo, the tigress was not interested in killing the bait.

**27**

Kalpur Singh had just finished his lunch. He promised his young wife he would be home before dinner, then made funny faces and cooed to his infant daughter as he walked out of his house. He untied his tethered cows and herded them up the road to a grassy field near the village. As the cattle grazed peacefully, Kalpur lay down in the shade of a large oak tree nearby. It was a bright, sunny day, and the pleasant temperature plus the effects of his noonday meal made him drowsy. Soon Kalpur dozed off.

An hour later, he was abruptly awakened by a covey of pheasants that fluttered from some dense brush thirty feet away, screaming their alarm. As Kalpur rubbed the sleep from his eyes, he heard the distinctive warning call of a langur monkey directly above him in the oak tree.

He had heard that the man-eater was active near Sem Village, some distance away, so he was not too concerned. However, since the langur's chattering was so incessant, Kalpur decided he'd better take a look around. As he stood up, he stretched his muscles. He peered up into the tree and saw the langur on a large branch. The monkey was looking toward the brush where the pheasants had been. Assuming the pheasants had alarmed the monkey, Kalpur checked to ensure his cows were all right, then lay back down again beneath the tree.

Moments later, the brush shook slightly; the man-eater had begun her stealthy approach. The tigress, annoyed by the chattering langur, looked up at it momentarily, then fixed her attention on her prey.

In three quick bounds, the tigress pounced on Kalpur, and within a minute, her throttling grip around his throat had choked the life from his body. The tigress then carried her meal off into the forest, where she could eat at her leisure. Kalpur's cows did not see the attack and continued to graze along the hillside without concern.

The following morning, word came to Jim and Ibby that a man was missing from Thak. They packed their gear and covered the four miles as quickly and prudently as possible. When they arrived in Thak, they checked the area where the man had been tending his cattle and found his hat and the tigress's pug marks.

Jim and Ibby tracked the man-eater for two hundred yards and came upon a pool of blood. They continued their pursuit a half-mile farther through thick underbrush, which took them nearly two hours to navigate. The two hunters followed the man-eater's trail to a rocky ledge, where Jim found part of the victim's remains.

Hoping the tigress would return to her kill, they constructed a *machan* in a tree overlooking the victim. Jim climbed into the *machan* at 4 P.M. and said good-bye to Ibby, who returned to the village with the servants. No sooner had Jim settled in his *machan* than he heard the alarm call of a small *kakar* (barking deer). Minutes later, he heard another alarm call from a sambar farther away.

Both deer were located in the same direction that Ibby and the servants had headed. Jim knew instantly what had happened. The tigress had abandoned her kill and was following Ibby and the others back to the village in hope of securing another victim.

"Be careful, Ibby!" Jim whispered. "Listen to the forest!"

Jim spent a very uneasy night worrying about his friend. Otherwise, everything was quiet. The next morning, Jim was elated when he saw Ibby returning along the trail with breakfast and hot tea. While Jim was eating and discussing the situation with Ibby, the relatives of the victim took the remains to the Sarda River for cremation. En route they chanted, *"Ram nam sat hai"* (The name of Rama is true) followed by the refrain, *"Satya bol gat hai"* (In truth lies salvation).

A few days later, the tigress killed a cow, over which Jim sat up at night in vain. Later, the man-eater killed one of the buffalo that had been tied up as bait. Again Jim and Ibby tracked it to a remote location in the forest, and again the crafty tigress was able to outsmart her pursuers.

By now the Ibbotsons had stayed as long as they could. While Bill was supervising the servants in preparation for their journey, Jean approached Jim with a concerned look.

"Will you be returning to Naini Tal tomorrow?"

"I can't," Jim sighed, "not until I get the man-eater."

Jean shook her head.

"No, Jim, please leave with us. It's much too dangerous!"

Jim could see the sincerity in her eyes. "I can't leave these people like this. My conscience wouldn't let me."

"I know," Jean replied. "But I'll only fret about your safety if you stay here. You should get some rest. You and Bill have been after the tigress for weeks now. You're both exhausted."

Jim bit his lower lip. Jean had a point, but he just couldn't abandon these helpless people.

"Last night I had a terrible dream that the man-eater killed you," she said. "When I awoke, I was frightened to death. I just don't know what I'd do if something happened to you."

"I know, Jean," Jim sighed and put his arm around her shoulders. She turned to him and grabbed his shirt collar.

"Then promise me you'll leave Thak," she almost demanded. Jim didn't want to make such a promise, but he hated seeing Jean so upset. And besides, he was awfully tired. He decided to give it one last shot.

"All right, I'll give it three more days. If I haven't destroyed it by then, I promise I'll pack it in and go home." Jean sighed in relief. "Thank you!" she said, then kissed him on the cheek.

Bill had their things all loaded up, and he came over to shake Jim's hand.

"Good luck, ol' boy," he said. "Bet Jean's got you on a return schedule already, doesn't she?" he grinned.

"We came to an understanding," Jim smiled good-naturedly.

"No man can refuse me, and that's the truth," Jean laughed,
clutching Bill's arm. Both Bill and Jim laughed.

As the Ibbotsons' entourage departed the village, Jean blew
Jim an exaggerated kiss. Jim smiled and waved, shaking his head.
He looked down at Robin and almost giggled, "What a minx, eh,
old fella? What a minx." Robin cocked his head and yapped in
agreement.

Jim tried every trick he knew to catch the man-eater over the
next three days, but nothing worked. Each animal was so different, and seemed to have its own distinct personality and crafti-
ness. Jim had to figure out what made each killer tick, and approach each hunt accordingly. He always expected the unexpected
from these man-eaters, and kept his wits about him at all times.
Still, this cat was being more than difficult, and it set Jim's spirits
low as he questioned his own abilities.

Nearly a month passed, and Jim was spent both physically
and emotionally. Despite his vast experience and success over the
years in destroying these beasts, hunting man-eaters never got any
easier, he realized. He had done all he could, but there was no
resolution to the problem in sight. He decided to pack it in, as he
had promised Jean, who he was sure was livid by this point that he
had not returned sooner. Jim bade farewell to the fear-stricken
villagers, as usual feeling terrible that he had not accomplished his
mission and had to leave them defenseless against such a clever,
ruthless killer.

Jim returned to Naini Tal on 8 November, and while he
was home, he was apprised of the man-eater's latest attack,
which occurred at Thak on 12 November. Following this attack, the villagers were so frightened that they fled and relocated in neighboring villages, intent on staying until the man-
eater was destroyed. When Jim heard this news, he knew he
must return. Despite the warnings and pleadings of his friends,

he packed up his gear and boarded the train on 22 November. He was settled in Chuka two days later.

Chuka was a small village two miles closer to Thak than Sem. Jim had arranged for three buffalo to be sent to Chuka, and they were waiting for him by the time he arrived. The villagers were ecstatic when they saw Jim return and felt confident he would be successful in ridding the beast from their lives. The children were also glad to see him, and crowded around him chanting, "Carpet Sahib!" (they had difficulty pronouncing his name, so "Corbett" came out "Carpet") and raised up their hands, hoping he had coins and candy to dispense among them. He always did.

Jim loved these children. Despite their abject poverty, they always seemed happy and carefree. They reminded Jim of his own youth. Oh, how he longed to return to his childhood—hunting with Kyle and Tommie, exploring for animals and flora in the forest, laughing at some of the stupid stunts his cousin Stephen always managed to pull. Being poor never seemed to matter back then.

The next morning, Jim took one of the buffaloes to Thak and tied it up where the attack had taken place on 12 November. When he entered the village, he was struck by the eerie silence. There were no sounds of human habitation whatsoever—just the usual sounds from the surrounding forest.

As Jim silently walked among the deserted houses, he noticed the tigress's pug marks prominently displayed along the dirt road and in front of the doorways to the houses. The villagers had fled in such a hurry, that some of the doors were left open. Jim gave those houses a wide berth in case the man-eater might be lurking inside.

After bedding down the buffalo with plenty of straw to eat, Jim headed back to Chuka. When he stopped at a stream to quench his thirst, a shiver ran through him as he noticed marks on the bank. The man-eater's paw prints were superimposed on the footprints he had left when he'd traveled to Thak only a couple of hours earlier.

Jim alerted his senses and clicked off the safety catch on his rifle. Cautiously, he continued his journey, treating every rock and bush along the trail as a potential ambush site. The tigress was in the area—of that there was no doubt. And the fact that it had not killed a human for days made Jim doubly cautious.

Jim arrived safely back at Chuka and advised everyone to be on their guard. The next morning he returned to Thak with another buffalo, and saw from tracks that the tigress had followed him back to Chuka the previous evening. Again he had to exercise extreme care.

After tying the second buffalo to a mango tree along the path, Jim checked on the buffalo he had left at Thak overnight. He found it grazing peacefully, but it must have had a very frightful night—the man-eater's pug marks were within a few feet of the buffalo, but the large cat had not taken advantage of the easy meal.

Jim returned to Chuka and took the third buffalo to Sem, tying it at a location the tigress had frequented when he and Ibby were tracking it. As at Chuka, the villagers at Sem were overjoyed to see Jim again, and his presence gave them the courage to sanitize their houses and resume a normal life until he had to return to Chuka for the night.

The next morning, Jim found all three buffalo undisturbed. He returned to Chuka and escorted the transplanted Thak residents back to their village so they could get some food and personal belongings that they had left behind when they fled.

Some of the village men suggested that Jim try sitting up over a goat, claiming the hill tigers prefer red goat to buffalo. To appease the villagers, Jim had his men tie a goat along the trail from Chuka to Thak and construct a rope *machan* for him in a tree overlooking the goat.

That night, discomfort from the ropes digging into his legs and the soaking from a fleeting rain shower only added to his frustration. When he had departed Naini Tal on the 22nd, he'd promised Maggie and the others that he would be gone only ten days.

To honor his promise, he had to depart on a train from Tanakpur no later than 30 November.

To add to his frustration, a large force of thousands of tree cutters and sawyers were working in the area, and had threatened to walk off the job if the man-eater was not destroyed. If Jim did not get a break soon, he would have to end his tiger-hunting career in bitter defeat.

At first light, Jim climbed down from the tree and returned to Chuka for breakfast and a hot bath. Later he went to Thak with his men to check on the buffalo. He found the first one intact, but as he approached the location of the second buffalo, two blue Himalayan magpies flew off in fright.

The presence of the magpies told Jim that the buffalo was dead and the tiger was not guarding the kill. Upon inspection of the carcass, Jim realized the buffalo had been killed by a cobra bite. However, the tigress had eaten a meal off the carcass sometime during the night. This gave Jim hope and bolstered his spirits. He had his men build a hasty *machan* while he stood guard and ate his biscuits and drank some hot tea, then sent the men back to Chuka.

That night the moon was full, showering the countryside with its shimmering brilliance. Jim could easily see the carcass and anything moving along the path. Soon the forest became very peaceful. Jim saw a sambar with her young one grazing near the path. The tranquillity of the setting warmed his heart.

Suddenly, a *kakar* in the direction of Thak belled its alarm. The sambar raised her head just as Jim heard a terrifying scream. It was the sound of a human in mortal agony, Jim was sure of it. The sound was three piercing cries, the last ending in a drawn-out note. The sambar and her young dashed off into the forest as soon as the cry began.

Jim's heart was pounding. His first impulse was to jump down from the tree and run to the village to assist. Then reason prevailed. The village was deserted, certainly. Everyone in the area knew the man-eater frequented Thak. Why would anyone in their right mind be in the village at night, knowing a killer was on the loose?

Maybe it was a looter, Jim surmised, someone who knew the village was empty and took advantage of the situation to steal from the vacant houses. If it was, Jim thought, then that poor soul had paid for his transgression in the most horrible manner imaginable.

The rest of the night was peaceful, and when Jim returned to Chuka the next morning, he told the village chief what he had heard.

"It could not have been a person," the wise, bearded old man said with certainty. "No one would be foolish enough to visit Thak at night as long as the man-eater is alive."

Jim spent the next night in the same *machan*. A cold wind blew from the north, chilling him to the bone. Once again, the tigress did not appear. When he returned to Chuka the following morning, he was met by several men from the labor camp who told him in great detail how the tigress had demonstrated in front of their camp throughout the night, roaring and snarling until the men cowered in fear.

This was Jim's last day. Frustrated beyond reason, he was resigned to catching the train on the following day, regardless. If he was unable to shoot the man-eater, someone else would have to take up the challenge. The thought of returning to Naini Tal in defeat soured his stomach with bile.

Jim decided to return to Thak with his men and two goats, and try one more time to attract the tigress. As they were walking along the path, Jim heard the tigress calling in the distance. He stopped and listened carefully, as Kunwah had taught him when he was young. The tigress called again. She was moving toward Thak! Jim was elated.

"Let's get moving!" he ordered his men as he quickened his stride.

The group continued toward Thak at a fast pace. Jim listened intently, but the tigress was quiet. Just as they were approaching the tree with the *machan*, a covey of pheasants went screaming from the brush next to the trail. Jim thought his heart had stopped for good!

As soon as the goats were tied near the tree, Jim escorted his men to a vacant house in Thak and left them with his .450-400 rifle. He quickly returned to the tree with his .275 Rigby and climbed into the *machan*. His heart was beating rapidly from the excitement and the promise that the tigress would soon appear.

At 5 P.M., Jim reluctantly climbed down from the tree, and with heavy feet, went to collect his men. The tigress had outsmarted him again. As he and his men trudged back to Chuka, Jim had never felt more depressed in his life. He heard the tigress calling off into the distance and could only shake his head. Just then, he remembered something!

It was prime mating season for tigers. Maybe, just maybe, the tigress was in estrus and searching for a mate. Maybe he could call her up to his location by imitating the call of a male tiger. He felt a brief surge of encouragement, but it quickly passed.

It was too late in the day to try such a foolish plan. Only a half-hour of daylight remained. If anything went wrong, he would be jeopardizing not only his own life but those of his men as well. As they continued down the trail, the plan kept entering Jim's mind.

The aging hunter was desperate. This was his last day to hunt the man-eater before he had to return to Naini Tal, leaving these helpless, gentle people in the grip of terror. He thought about asking his men for their opinion, but knew their answer would favor their own skins. No, he would have to make this decision on his own.

Jim stopped along the trail and handed his rifle to one of his men. Filling his lungs to capacity, he bellowed the loud, moaning sound of an amorous male tiger. He hoped it would be convincing. Silence fell over the area for the next few minutes, then Jim repeated the call: *"Aaooaarr!"* Instantly, the tigress returned his call, and for the next five minutes, Jim and the tigress called back and forth. From the location of the tigress's calls, Jim could tell it was on the move—toward them. He examined the immediate area to determine how the pending saga might unfold.

They were on an open, grassy knoll surrounded on two sides by rocky embankments. Behind them was a sharp drop-off, making access for retreat impossible. To their front was the tigress, and partially open terrain through which it would have to approach them. That large, rectangular area contained rocks, grassy areas, clumps of brush, and occasional trees for about eighty yards, terminating at the edge of the forest.

Jim responded again to the tigress's call, and began looking for a vantage point from which to shoot the beast if it came into sight. The only place of concealment in the immediate area was a large boulder four feet high that abutted the rocky embankment on the side. Not a great place to hide, but it would have to suffice.

Jim placed his men and the goats on the ground behind the boulder. He leaned against it and, with one foot resting on a small ledge near the ground, was able to perch his .450-400 double-barreled rifle over the top of the boulder.

He turned around to see his men directly behind and slightly below him, crouched down facing each other with a look of terror on their faces. Knowing a man-eating tigress was rapidly approaching their position and darkness was only minutes away, Jim shared their horror.

The die was cast. There was no retreat from the terrible situation in which Jim had placed his men. He felt awful, but yet encouraged that he might finally get a chance to kill the dreadful beast that had been spreading terror throughout the area for years.

The tigress called again. Jim estimated it was about two hundred yards to his front and could make the distance to them in a few minutes. He bellowed another call so the tigress could accurately locate their position.

He then checked his rifle to ensure both barrels were loaded and the safety was off. Just then, he recalled seeing a dented cartridge while inspecting his equipment two days earlier. *Did I remember to throw it away?* he wondered. The thought that it might now be inside one of the chambers sent a chill down his spine.

He could now hear the tigress grunting as it moved through the bushes to his front, anxious to join its "mate." He heard more noise and saw some bushes flutter. But he could not see the tiger, which caused him considerable consternation. Then complete silence washed over the area—no chitals barking, no langur monkeys calling out their alarm, no magpies chirping their warning. Nothing but silence!

*"RRROOARRR!"* With a noise that nearly stopped Jim's heart, the tigress bellowed its call from the other side of the rocky embankment directly to his right. He could smell the tigress's pungent breath, caused by decaying flesh.

Jim had never been so frightened. Icy fingers of fear tightened the muscles in his neck and shoulders. He waited nervously. He had not expected the tigress to approach from that direction, and if she scrambled over the embankment toward them, he would have a very difficult shot.

The tigress sucked air into its lungs and called out again. The roar was so deafening and frightful that Jim thought his men would panic and run away screaming. Were it not for the rifle he was holding, he might have felt compelled to take flight also. The tigress had worked herself into a fury over her desire to join a mate. Jim recalled the time a tigress in heat had caused a road a short distance from his home to be closed, ferociously attacking anything and anybody for an entire week until she was finally joined by a mate.

Jim realized this tigress was confused and frustrated, and was waiting for another call to get its bearings. Fortunately, the wind was blowing from his front, making it impossible for the tigress to pick up human scent. Time was running out. Jim had only a few more minutes before the cloak of darkness would put them at the mercy of the man-eater.

Quietly filling his lungs, Jim cupped his mouth and emitted one final soft, moaning call. He froze, not knowing what to expect next. He fervently hoped his call was convincing enough to bring the tigress out into the open so he could get a shot at it. And yet at the same time he also hoped the tigress would not appear—would instead become suspicious and slink back into the darkening forest. He was having second thoughts about confronting the killer here under these conditions.

Jim could now hear the tigress grunting her frustration while prancing through the thick brush only ten feet to his front. He caught a fleeting glimpse of her as she passed between two bushes. He heard her tramping around in the brush some more, and then she finally emerged, staring right into Jim's face, and stopped dead in her tracks.

Once again Jim felt the cool, sour sweat of fear seeping through his body. The tigress was only seven feet to his front, standing in a slight depression. He did not want to risk a head shot, but the tigress was giving him no other option. Aiming just below its right eye, Jim squeezed the trigger, followed immediately by the second trigger.

What happened next can only be described as chaos and hysteria. The recoil from the rifle knocked Jim off the boulder onto his men and the goats. Not knowing whether the tigress was alive or dead, he quickly untangled himself from his men, snatched the .275 from his bearer's hands, and leaped to a position from which he hoped to see the man-eater.

Purple shadows crept along the ground, limiting Jim's vision. But the darkness did not hide his adversary. The beast lay dead on the ground, its head resting against the boulder. The first bullet had hit the man-eater exactly where Jim had aimed, and the second one caught it in the throat.

Jim saw that the tiger was no longer breathing and, convinced it was finished, leaned against the boulder to steady his legs. He then reached for a well-deserved cigarette to quiet his screaming nerves. Just then, he felt the pain in his jaw caused by the impact from his rifle's recoil. He placed his hand on the swollen wound.

"Sahib?" his bearer asked quietly.

"I'm all right. It's finished." Knowing that the area was now safe, Jim fired his rifle five times in succession to let everyone within hearing distance know that the man-eater was dead. He then had his men cut two saplings while he went back to the village to round up enough men and rope to haul the tiger.

Jim could not feel his feet touch the ground as he walked down the dark path to Chuka. Not only did he no longer have to fear being attacked by the man-eater, but he was positively elated by having destroyed the menace that had been terrorizing these villagers for so long.

Jim thought, *If the greatest happiness anyone can experience is the sudden cessation of pain, then the second greatest happiness is the sudden cessation of fear.*

Having heard Jim's shots, villagers from all over the area were now heading up the path. Only minutes earlier, wild horses could not have dragged these people from their homes, but now they were walking through the dark forest without fear.

Jim celebrated the success with the villagers and told the Thak residents they could now return to their homes. Later, as he skinned the tigress with his knife next to a roaring bonfire, he noticed the gunshot wounds in its shoulder that had caused it to become a man-eater.

Jim bathed and dressed for his return home while the villagers continued to revel in their happiness. He said his farewells to the joyful people, then began the twenty-mile walk to the train station at Tanakpur. As he proceeded along the trail with his men in file behind him, he looked down at Robin and said, "I guess we're both getting too old for this nonsense, aren't we, fella?"

Robin looked up, then barked his concurrence.

During World War II, Jim again served the Crown by organizing a civil pioneer corps of Kumaon volunteers. His title
was Deputy Military Vice-President of the District Soldiers Board.

Following a serious bout of tick fever, from which Maggie
nursed him back to health, Jim was asked to train British soldiers
in jungle warfare at a special camp in central India; these men
were destined to fight the Japanese in neighboring Burma. Jim
was a natural for the position and excelled at training his charges.
He taught them everything he knew about how to survive in the
jungle—what plants were edible and how to find them; how to
signal for help without alerting enemy soldiers within earshot; how
to track the enemy in the jungle; how to evade the enemy and
avoid capture; and how to make lethal weapons for hunting and
self-defense. At the conclusion of the war, Jim, by then a lieutenant colonel, returned home to Maggie, Robin, and tranquillity—
for a short while.

As much as Jim detested politics, he could no longer ignore
the Indian quest for independence from British rule. Skirmishes
instigated by Indian malcontents against the British were becoming more frequent, and Jim could sense the growing current of
unity among the native population. The British government had
made concessions over the years, but in most cases they were too
little and too late.

The Indian campaign for "home rule" had spread rapidly
throughout the country, recruiting millions of followers. As a means

of demonstrating against British rule, many Indians resigned from
their government jobs and boycotted British goods. Indian children were removed from government schools by their parents,
and there was a growing reluctance to pay taxes to the British
government. In an effort to combat this growing rebellion, British
authorities cracked down more harshly on the dissidents. This
"solution" only resulted in more dissidence and open rebellion.

Fearing for their safety, many British, Americans, and other
Europeans elected to stay out of India until order was restored.
Many British officials stationed in India sent their families back to
England or some other country where they would be safe. Although Jim truly loved India and regarded it as his homeland, deep
down he knew that someday he would have to leave the country
of his birth.

Jim had divested his holdings in Africa several years earlier at a tidy profit. His hunch concerning coffee had paid off.
Demand had grown significantly, and profits grew correspondingly. However, he tired of the time-consuming journeys and
finally sold his holdings.

Naini Tal had grown considerably over the years and was
rapidly becoming a prosperous settlement. When Jim was born,
the population of Naini Tal had been no more than a few thousand.
Nestled in the Himalayan foothills, its beauty and climate were
unsurpassed. The community was surrounded by lushly forested
hills containing numerous crystal-clear lakes and ponds fed by
streams originating high in the snowcapped mountains to the north.
Word spread quickly, and by 1947 the populace was approaching
50,000 full-time residents. People vacationing in Naini Tal to escape the hot summer months in the lowlands bolstered the population by several thousand more. The town's growth was a boon to
every property owner and retail establishment in the area, and the
value of the Corbett family's Gurney House increased correspondingly.

Jim was at the Gurney house writing memoirs of his hunting
experiences when he looked out the window to see two Indian
women approaching. As they got closer, he thought he recognized one of them. There was something about her face that re-

minded Jim of his childhood. When the women stepped onto his front porch, Jim shuddered with excitement. It was Punatii!

He had not seen her since he was sixteen, when she left for Moradabad to become the maharaja's wife. Of course, he had heard about her from time to time over the years from her father, but he never expected to see her again. When he greeted her at the door, he was dumbstruck.

"Hello, Jim," Punatii said with a smile. Her face was still radiant like a young girl's, and her dark eyes housed a wealth of stories.

"Punatii? I can't believe it! What a wonderful surprise! Please come in."

Punatii ordered her servant to wait outside as she entered and took a seat at the table. Jim could barely keep himself from staring at her. She was still quite beautiful. He got her a cup of tea and sat down.

"Is Maggie at home?" she asked as she sipped from her cup.

"No, she went to the market this morning, but she'll be back in a few hours—gosh, she'd love to see you!"

"That would be nice."

Jim fumbled to make conversation. So what brings you here? Are you visiting your father?"

"I live with my father now. The maharaja, my husband, died last year. Afterward, his eldest son would not allow me to remain in Moradabad, so I came to my father's estate. My sister also lives with me."

Jim was intrigued. "I'm sorry about your husband—what an awful ordeal it must have been."

Punatii shrugged her shoulders and smiled somewhat devilishly. She whispered low over her teacup to Jim. "It wasn't so bad. My husband was a very old man, and not terribly kind." She laughed lightly. "I think I had my bags packed before his son finished knocking on my chamber door!"

Jim's jaw dropped, and they both broke into hearty laughter.

"So how have you and your dear sister been these many years?" Punatii asked, still giggling.

Jim knew he couldn't fit forty years into several minutes, so he gave her the basics, and told a few amusing tiger tales.

"I am surprised you still walk the earth, Jim," she said. "You must have the gods on your side."

"Well, they certainly aren't on my payroll—must be they can't stand overbearing cats!"

They laughed again. Jim felt so comfortable with Punatii, a peace he hadn't felt in a long time. Now that the hunts were officially over, another part of himself, a part that had been pushed aside by his passion for the hunt, was awakening. He stared at the beautiful woman at his table.

"What are your plans?" he asked nonchalantly as he poured her more tea, then walked toward the stove to get more hot water.

"I am a follower of Mahatma Gandhi. I recruit members in our district."

Jim spun around. "Punatii! You must be careful." He looked quickly out the window to see who was around, "If the British authorities find out . . ."

"Don't worry, Jim," she said, "I don't believe in violence, and neither does Gandhi. He is a peace-loving man who advocates only passive resistance to the British. He denounces those factions that use violent means to obtain independence. When I met Gandhi four years ago, I became very impressed with his ideas. He is very religious, spending most of his time praying, meditating, and fasting. He encourages his followers to return to the old ways and a simpler lifestyle. You should listen to what he says, Jim. He dresses like a peasant, but my people love him as though he was a king. He has wonderful ideas for India, after we win our independence. And I want to be part of that process—building a new, free India."

Jim sat in silence for several seconds, trying to digest what he had just heard. "I know all about Gandhi and what he is trying to do. What I don't understand is why so many Indians despise the British after all we've done to help your people. I mean, we've established a workable government, built roads, established a good educational system, provided jobs, and bolstered your economy. Why can't you appreciate everything the British have done?"

"Jim," Punatii answered, "you're looking at this from only your side. We do appreciate the British for bringing us into the modern world. However, our cultures are so different, and we want to travel our own path. The British treat us like children, and believe we will always need their protection and guidance. But children eventually grow up and want to be independent—to make their own decisions and to follow their own destiny. Don't you see, Jim? To us, the British are like the man-eating tiger. Just like the villagers who wish to rid themselves of the tiger's tyranny, so we wish to end British tyranny. Every living thing in our world wants to be free, and we're no different. Oh, Jim, I do hope you understand."

"I understand," Jim acknowledged somberly. "But I'm concerned about your safety. Don't you realize you could be imprisoned for your actions?"

"I'll have to take that chance. Mahatma Gandhi has been imprisoned many times in his life, yet his strong belief in freedom and justice permits him to endure man's evil treatment. I hope that someday I will be as strong as Gandhi."

Jim stared at Punatii speechless. She continued, "Jim, the real reason I came to see you is to warn you and Maggie."

Jim looked perplexed. "Warn us about what?"

"There are some factions who believe they can obtain their objectives only through violence. Some of these people live in Naini Tal District. They are fanatics and will stop at nothing. Your life, and Maggie's, might be in danger."

"That's absurd! We've helped these villagers our entire lives. I can't believe they would harbor any intent to harm us."

"What you say is true," continued Punatii, "but there are some who do not know you or what you and Maggie have done for our people. These are the ones I'm referring to. They see you as British, and to them, all British should be treated the same—with violence. Please, Jim, I think you and Maggie should leave India for a while—just until this violence goes away. I don't want to see either of you hurt."

"I appreciate your concern, but we haven't done anything wrong. I refuse to run away from my homeland because of some radicals who dislike the British."

"Please, Jim," Punatii pleaded, "think about what I've said. Talk to Maggie before you decide anything. I must go now."

As Punatii walked from the house, Jim felt angry and hurt—betrayed by the people to whom he and Maggie had devoted their lives.

Two months after Punatii's visit, Jim noticed Robin's health beginning to deteriorate. His faithful companion was eighteen years old, and life's hardships were taking their toll. The spaniel was suffering from acute arthritis as well as old age, and it was difficult for him to get up from his bed.

Maggie, feeling sorry for Robin, advised Jim to put him to sleep. Jim refused. He loved his dog dearly and held onto any thread of hope that Robin would somehow miraculously recover from his many ailments. Whenever Robin wanted to leave his bed, Jim carried him outside. Often he held Robin on his lap as he sat in the rocking chair on the porch, petting him while reminiscing about their many adventures together hunting wild game. Robin looked into Jim's eyes with his own sad, bulging eyes and licked Jim's hand as he talked. On extremely hot days, Jim carried Robin to a large tree in the garden and placed him in his favorite shady spot.

One day, as Jim was compiling notes about his and Robin's pursuit of the Thak man-eater, he got up from his chair and walked to the kitchen for a glass of water. As he went by Robin, he observed him sleeping comfortably on his bed. When Jim returned from the kitchen, Robin had rolled onto his side and was no longer breathing.

When Maggie returned home, she found Jim sitting in the rocker on the porch, holding Robin's lifeless body in his arms and gently stroking his head. When she saw the sadness in Jim's eyes, she knew instantly what had happened.

"Oh, Jim," Maggie sighed, placing her hand on Jim's shoulder, "I'm so sorry!"

Jim continued staring at the forest and the foothills beyond and whispered, "God, if you're really there . . . take care of the old chap, will you? I would greatly appreciate it." He got up and carried Robin out to the garden and began digging the bed where his trusted friend and companion would sleep in peace.

**29**

Jim had told Maggie of his conversation he had with Punatii and of Punatii's warning to leave the country. Maggie, like Jim, did not want to leave their homeland. She was comfortable with her lifestyle and enjoyed administering first-aid treatment to her village friends from their house. Maggie was sixty-five years old and did not relish the idea of starting a new life in another country. She had heard from others that violence against the British was escalating in India, but hoped that it would not affect their small, peaceful community.

It was 10 P.M., and Jim had just completed the final touches to a chapter of his book. Maggie had already retired for the evening. Trying not to disturb her, he quietly walked to his bedroom and prepared himself for a comfortable night's rest. As he lay in his overstuffed bed, he thought about all the times he had spent in the forested hills searching for man-eaters. Gone were the days of hardship and sleepless nights sitting up over goats and buffalo in an uncomfortable *machan*, waiting patiently for an unsuspecting tiger or leopard to appear. No longer did he have to endure the night's bitter chill or being soaked to the skin by a monsoon storm. Now he could spend his golden years in comfort, working in his garden and writing his memoirs. Occasionally, he would still go on a hunt. But it would be of his own choosing and after game that did not want to attack and eat him. Jim fell asleep.

At 2 A.M., Jim suddenly awoke. He thought he heard a noise, some sort of shuffling sound. He gazed around the room, trying to rub the sleep from his eyes with his hand. As his eyes began to focus, he saw a tall, dark object standing next to his bed. In a panic, he lunged for his pistol, which he kept on the nightstand. Simultaneously, he felt a sharp pain as something cracked his skull and he fell into unconsciousness.

"Englishman! Englishman!" Jim heard the voice say as he regained his senses.

"Maggie!" Jim shouted, wondering what had happened to his sister. Then he heard Maggie's muffled sobs coming from across the dark room. "What's going on?"

"Your sister is fine," the stranger replied. "She is tied up like you are and has a cloth in her mouth."

"Who are you, and what do you want?" Jim tried desperately to loosen the rope that bound his hands to the back of the chair on which he was sitting. "Take what you want, but please don't hurt my sister!"

"We're not interested in robbing you," the man continued. "We want you to leave our country . . . NOW! Your friend has protected you in the past, but she has been . . . how do you say . . . replaced." A sinister chuckle followed. "Her peaceful ways are ineffective, as are her leader's. This is our first and only warning to you. You are lucky to even get that. It is only because of your help to these townspeople that your throats have not been slit already! You must leave by morning or die."

"Yes, all right." Jim said. "But please, tell me what happened to Punatii."

The mysterious man snickered. "She met with an unfortunate accident. You can attend her cremation tomorrow if you like." The man laughed, and slapped Jim on the back.

Jim began to curse the man, then another one placed a rag in Jim's mouth and tied it securely behind his head. His eyes were on fire. Angry tears soaked his cheeks as the band of men patted each other on the back and walked off into the night chanting a song of victory.

The next morning, their servants found Jim and Maggie tied to the chairs. When they were released, Maggie ran to Jim's arms and wept hysterically.

"I'm so frightened! They could have killed us!"

"I know," Jim said softly while holding her tight. "I know."

Word spread quickly concerning Punatii's death. She was highly revered throughout the area, and now no one felt safe from these "intruders of the night." Many Indians suspected that the British were responsible for Punatii's death, adding more distrust and hatred to an already volatile situation. Even the villagers, who were not politically involved, feared for their lives. Anxiety was running rampant over the anticipated violence that was soon to come.

That afternoon, Jim and Maggie attended Punatii's cremation ceremony, held at a nearby stream, a tributary to the Ganges River. Punatii's involvement with Gandhi's movement was well known among British authorities, and Jim noticed the absence of British folk at the ceremony. As the raging fire engulfed Punatii's funeral pyre, Jim put his arm around Maggie and said, "It's time to leave." Maggie looked into Jim's eyes and nodded.

Two days later, Jim and Maggie were loading their luggage and possessions into their horse-drawn carriage and wagon while the villagers looked on with sadness in their eyes. They did not want Jim and Maggie to leave. They had relied on the Corbetts' advice and assistance throughout most of their lives, and now they had to learn to do without. They were afraid to face life on their own.

Jim and Maggie had executed documents bequeathing to their faithful servants their property at Kaladhungi, as well as their livestock and other possessions that they could not take with them. Additionally, they pledged to continue paying the property tax for as long as they lived—a promise that was never broken. Only several villagers and a few close friends knew of their departure. Jim and Maggie wanted it that way.

As Jim climbed into the carriage, he looked back one last time at the town where he grew up, at the forested hills beyond where he derived so much enjoyment hunting and hiking, and at the snowcapped peaks of the majestic Himalayas far off in the distance, highlighted against the sapphire blue sky. Tears stung his eyes as he waved farewell to the people and the land he loved so dearly. He knew he would never again see their faces, and it made him heartsick, but the thought that his ears would never again hear the tiger's roar—that was like a shot in the gut. He tipped his hat one last time, and closed his eyes. *Only here, in my mind's eye, will I see the great cats now,* he told himself, *only here.*

# BIBLIOGRAPHY

Barnes, Simon. *Tiger!* New York: St. Martin's Press, 1994.

Baze, William. *Tiger, Tiger.* London: Elek Books Ltd., 1957.

Booth, Martin. *Carpet Sahib.* London: Oxford University Press, 1991

Braddon, Sir E. *Thirty Years of Shikar.* London: William Blackwood & Sons, 1895.

Channing, Mark. *India Mosaic.* London: J.B. Lippincott Co., 1936.

Corbett, Jim. *Jungle Lore.* London: Oxford University Press, 1953.

———. *Man-eaters of Kumaon.* London: Oxford University Press, 1946.

———. *Man-eaters of India.* London: Oxford University Press, 1957.

———. *My India.* London: Oxford University Press, 1952.

*Current Biography Yearbook.* New York: H.W. Wilson Co.,1946 & 1955.

*Dictionary of National Biography D.N.B. 1951-1960.* London: Oxford University Press.

Kala, D.C. *Jim Corbett of Kumaon.* New Delhi: Ankur Publishing House, 1979.

Powell, Colonel A. N. W. *Call of the Tiger.* London: Robert Hale Ltd., 1957.

Scott, Jack Denton. *Forests of the Night.* New York: Rinehart & Co., Inc., 1959.

Singh, Colonel Kesri. *The Tiger of Rajasthan.* London: Robert Hale Ltd., 1959.

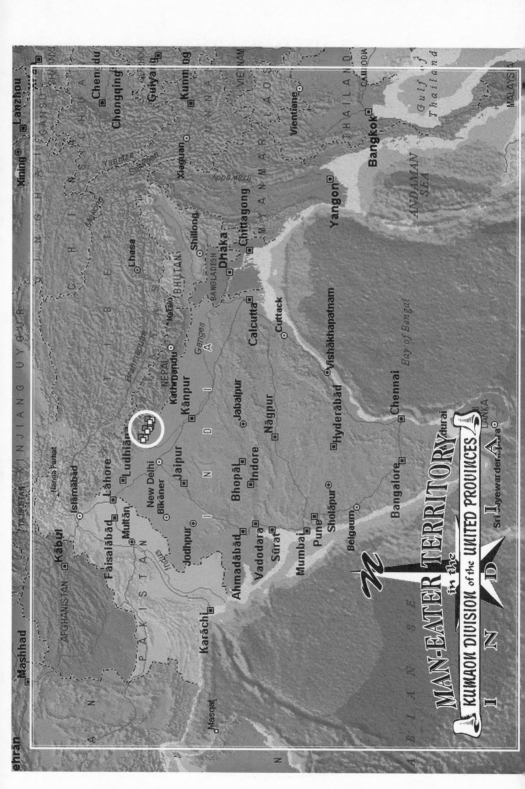

MAN-EATER TERRITORY in the KUMAON DIVISION of the UNITED PROVINCES
I N D I A